A Treasury Of
AMISH QUILTS

Center Square
1914 • Wool • 70 x 74 • Lancaster Co., Pennsylvania • Private collection.
Grape leaves and clusters of tiny round grapes adorn this red inner border. The date "1914" is neatly quilted in the lower right hand corner. The exceptional quality of workmanship shown here is typical of early Lancaster Co. quilts.

A TREASURY OF
AMISH QUILTS

Rachel and Kenneth Pellman

Good Books
Intercourse, Pennsylvania 17534

Acknowledgements

We wish to thank many people for helping to make this book a reality. Numerous conversations and interviews over the years have contributed vital information to this project. We especially thank Dr. Patricia Herr, Rebecca Haarer, Connie Hayes, Julie Silber, Darwin Bearley, David Pottinger, Joel and Kate Kopp, Steve Scott, Elizabeth Warren, Daniel and Kathryn McCauley, Jill and Henry Barber and Barbara Janos for the insight and knowledge they passed on to us. We appreciate equally the help of those persons within the various Amish communities who wish to remain anonymous. The quilting stories appeared in *Die Botschaft*, Box 807, Lancaster, PA 17603.

Additionally, we are most grateful to all the people who so willingly allowed us to photograph their quilt treasures. Without their kindness, the beauty of this book would pale.

All photography by Jonathan Charles except: Fred Wilson, 6, 8; Peter Zimberg, 7, Kenneth Pellman 9, 54, 77; Richard Reinhold, 55 (top), 76 (top); David Lauver, 55 (Bottom), 102; Lee Snider, 76 (Bottom), 103.

Design by Cheryl A. Benner
A Treasury of Amish Quilts
© 1990 by Good Books, Intercourse, PA 17534
International Standard Book Number: 1-56148-000-2
Library of Congress Catalog Card Number: 90-82488

Library of Congress Cataloging-in-Publication Data

Pellman, Rachel T. (Rachel Thomas)
   A treasury of Amish quilts / Rachel and Kenneth
Pellman.

      p.   cm.
   Includes bibliographical references and index.
   ISBN 1-56148-000-2 ; $19.95
    1. Quilts, Amish—Catalogs. I. Pellman, Kenneth,
   1952-
II. Title.
NK9112.P443 1990   90-82488
746.9'7'088287—dc20   CIP

TABLE OF CONTENTS

ABOUT AMISH QUILTS

We have long been drawn to the wonder of Amish quilts. Their vibrant color, their energy of design, their fields of quilting are arresting creative expressions. Born out of austere and disciplined communities, these quilts seem to hold secrets about life, tradition and inspiration.

We write from Lancaster County, Pennsylvania, home of the second largest community of Old Order Amish in the world. It is the birthplace, too, of quilt masterpieces. What has contributed to this burst of artistry? Why have these reserved people created such bold designs of startling colors?

The "Golden Years" of Amish Quilts

The most striking and distinctive Amish quilts were made between the late 1800s and 1940. Made with only solid color fabrics, these quilts are distinguished, as well, for their color arrangement, precise piecework and exquisite quilting. By the late 1800s, Amish communities throughout Pennsylvania, Ohio and Indiana were finally well established. Not all of a family's energy was required for surviving in the wilderness, as had been true in earlier years. In addition, the Amish church itself had developed a clearer identity with a more defined way of living for its members.

In fact, quilts from different Amish communities show characteristics of the areas from which they come. These distinctives are due to differing economic conditions, the amount of interchange the Amish had with the larger world and varying levels of church district influence. While those factors help identify an antique quilt's origin, another social factor may confuse that process. Amish communities did not, and do not now, live in isolation from each other. Members have always visited extensively from community to community. With that kind of interchange has come much sharing of ideas and influence.

The most artistic antique Amish quilts speak a language of strength and simplicity, no matter their community of origin. Their piecing and color are graphically strong; their quilting is full, balancing the starkness of the design. One needs to look at the cultural and spiritual backgrounds out of which these bedcovers come to better understand their vitality.

Why Has Quilting Thrived Among the Amish?

Many of the same dynamics are at work today in Old Order Amish communities as were in the years between 1890 and 1940. What are those impulses, those forces

Hot weather cannot deter a quilting. The frame is taken outside where the socializing and quilting continue.

Children are cherished; considered a gift from God.

that combine to form such powerful beauty?

1. The work ethic is strong among the Amish. Adults spend little time in non-productive pastimes. Young children may play, imagine and explore, but at an early age they are given responsibilities and chores. Quilting provides women a productive, yet enjoyable diversion from routine homemaking activities.

2. Hand-in-hand with their high regard for work is the Amish respect for doing jobs well. That ideal is evident in their quiltmaking. There are always exceptions, but generally Amish women are excellent craftspersons, sewing and quilting with great care.

3. The practical Amish mentality has little room for art without some useful purpose. That does not mean that the Amish way of life stifles creative spirits. Instead, it channels creativity into paths that are useful within the community boundaries. Quilts fit that arena. They are a creative venture that is useful; they are a marriage of beauty and utility.

4. Quiltings reinforce the social fabric of the Amish community. In a world where telephones are prohibited in the home, social connections depend on visiting and the mail. Visiting is not limited to friends and neighbors, but happens also within families. In one Amish family with whom we are friends, two daughters were married in the past two years. Each young woman made quilts to take with her as she established her own home. When we would see Sarah in the weeks before the weddings we would ask what she planned to do that day.

Regularly she would say, "The girls and I are going to quilt today." Not only were they making a bed cover; Sarah and her daughters were sitting together for the day, talking with each other about life and the upcoming marriages. Quilting provided the occasion for a mother to pass on to her daughters the faith community's expectations about their new roles as wives.

5. Quilts are an acceptable way to show caring in a society that expresses affection with great restraint. Thousands of minute quilting stitches speak of love. The gentle discipline of piecing reminds both the maker and the recipient of the deep bonds that connect them.

We particularly remembered that aspect of quiltmaking after a recent conversation with Leah, an Old Order Amish neighbor of ours. Leah, whose slight, somewhat frail look belies the stamina within her, lives with her adult son Ben, who is mentally handicapped and requires special attention to keep him occupied. Because Leah's husband is no longer living, Ben's care is her responsibility, a sizable task for this tiny elderly woman. Sewing is a favorite pastime for both Leah and Ben, despite the fact that they must use a treadle sewing machine, since their home has no electricity, as is the practice among the Amish.

One day as Leah was going by, we asked how she was feeling, knowing that she was having some health problems. Her reply was that she was "Good," although "Pretty tired," since she had spent all morning on her knees operating the sewing machine treadle with her hands so Ben could sew his quilt top together. Ben had cross-stitched patches for a quilt top but lacked the co-ordination to run the treadle with his feet while using his hands to guide the patches under the presser foot.

Making patches was a useful and enjoyable project for Ben. The finished cover gives him a sense of accom-plishment each time it is used. Putting the quilt together was Leah's way of conveying to Ben the value of work and the reward of doing a job well. She was willing to invest hours of patience and teaching to help Ben re-alize her caring for him, as well as the pleasure of a com-pleted quilt.

What Characterizes Antique Amish Quilts?

Quilts made by Amish women today vary little, for the most part, from those made by general society. It is the early Amish quilts, those made from the late 19th century and into the mid-20th century, that represent a distinctive body of quilts. They are characterized by bold, solid colors put together in stark, geometric shapes and lavished with tiny, precise quilting stitches.

A good treadle sewing machine at a country auction is worth considering.

The fabrics of these old quilts were generally the fab-rics used in Amish clothing. Cottons and wools pre-dominate. Their colors are the deep rich colors of Amish clothing, often highlighted by the use of black. The colors worn by the Amish during this period usually included only half the spectrum of the color wheel, ranging from green to, and including, darker shades of red. Bright reds, oranges and yellows, though they ap-

pear occasionally in quilts, were generally avoided in clothing. How did these forbidden colors creep into patchwork? One woman explained the use of bright red in her quilt, "There were peddlers who visited our area and, after learning to know their clientele, would make fabric bundles for us." These bright fabrics were in those bundles. Since they could not be used for clothing, nor could the buyers bear to throw them away, they began to appear in quilt tops, as well as garment linings and facings.

Old Amish quilts can be grouped into several main categories. From Lancaster County, Pennsylvania, come some of the oldest and best examples of Amish quiltmaking. Three patterns in particular are associated almost exclusively with that area: the Center Diamond, Bars, and Sunshine and Shadow. These quilts were most often made of fine wools. The large pieces of fabric needed to execute the patterns would indicate that some fabrics were purchased specifically for quilts. Because the Lancaster County Amish were among the first Amish settlements, they became financially secure at an earlier point than those settlements further west and so could afford to be more extravagant with quilt fab-rics. The Center Diamond pattern is sometimes re-ferred to by Amish women as a "Cape quilt." That name comes from the fact that dresses wore out but capes seldom did. Capes (an additional loose garment fitting over the bodice of the dress for the purpose of modesty) were triangular in shape and could be used to fill in the corners of the Center Diamond pattern. Capes were also cut up for use in Sunshine and Shadow quilts.

The large expanses of solid fabric in the Center Dia-mond and Bars quilts seemed to inspire a burst of en-ergy in quilters. These spaces were covered with a va-riety of delicate quilting designs, including intricate feather circles and plumes, grape leaves with tiny spher-ical grapes, pumpkin seeds and abundant, close cros-shatching. Characteristically wide borders provided more space for fine quilting. All in all, Lancaster County Amish quilts excel in both visual and workmanship quality.

Quilts from the Amish settlements of Mifflin County, Pennsylvania, are different from Lancaster County quilts in both color and pattern. Colors varied from rather dull combinations of blues, purples and browns from the most conservative group to gaudy combina-tions that included hot pink, bright yellows and vibrant blue from the less conservative churches. Patterns var-ied greatly, but many can be traced to some version of the basic Four-Patch or Nine-Patch design. Fabrics were primarily cottons with some wools. Borders were less wide than on Lancaster quilts and quilting motifs tended to be less elaborate.

Midwestern Amish quilts broadened the spectrum of pattern choices. When migrating from the East and resettling in a new area, the Amish had more interaction with the outside world. Quilts from the large Amish communities of Ohio and Indiana indicate that there was more trading of patterns among themselves and with their non-Amish neighbors. In spite of that, these quilts stand apart because they consistently avoided the use of any printed fabrics. Patchwork designs were executed in solid colors and placed on dark fields, often black or shades of blue. Quilting motifs on midwestern quilts tended to be cables, floral motifs, fan and straight lines.

The inner lining of antique quilts was much flatter than the polyester batting so prevalent today. Sometimes a cotton batting was used; sometimes simply an old blanket or some other additional layer of fabric was put between the top and bottom layers. Cotton batting required a lot of quilting to secure the batt and keep it from shifting or becoming lumpy with use. However, the amount and intricacy of the quilting on these antique masterpieces far exceed what was needed for utilitarian purposes. Clearly that quilting served a purpose beyond doing its job of keeping the quiltmaker's family warmly covered.

Contemporary Amish Quilts

Amish quilts today are much less distinctive. Although printed fabrics are still not used in clothing, prints are frequently purchased for use in quilts. Quilting stitches are generally less abundant and less fine than on early quilts. That has happened partly because polyester batting is used today. It retains its shape and requires less quilting to keep it in place. Less abundant, fine stitching is done today, also, because many Amish quilts are made to sell. It is simply not financially practical to invest as much time and energy in the quilting process.

The marketing of Amish quilts has greatly affected the type of quilts Amish quiltmakers produce. Instead of starting with available fabrics left over from home sewing, supplemented with a few purchased pieces, Amish women buy fabrics specifically to make a particular quilt in a particular color. That requires the fabrics to be color coordinated according to general society's sense of what is pleasing. This consciousness of "appropriate" color coordination has undone the naive use of color so evident in the best early Amish quilts. Much of the magic in those old Amish quilts is their unusual, often shocking combinations of intense colors. These

Vine-ripened strawberries from the garden are a delightful treat.

stark contrasts were achieved largely because the women piecing them did so without preconceived ideas of what "went together" and what didn't. In the Amish world, one need not be concerned with coordinating socks, tops, skirts and shoes. Accessories are not used. For all practical purposes, any article of clothing in an Amish person's wardrobe can be worn with any other piece.

Homes are traditionally devoid of upholstered furniture. Carpets are generally rag rugs, and window treatments are usually a simple pull blind. Walls are most often painted a pale blue or green color. There is no need to color coordinate one's living space. In a world where neither clothing nor home furnishings need to be matched, the eye is free to see color in a more primal sense. One woman who chose to leave the Old Order church as an adult explained her difficulty in learning to dress in a non-Amish way. She felt no confidence in planning a wardrobe and worked hard to develop a sense of what to wear with what.

The finest old quilts were not a random selection of fabrics; they were clearly planned, but they were laid out without regard for what was "right" or "wrong" in terms of color theory. They were done without inhibitions. The Amish approach to color was new and fresh—something we modern persons often stumble over because we "know" too much. This innocence, applied to quiltmaking, has produced a body of quilts with a timeless beauty. The quilts come from a community of persons committed to simplicity and nonconformity. These values are evident in their quilts, which become a bridge for many of us to gain a greater understanding of the Amish way of life.

CENTER DIAMOND

Center Diamond
Circa 1900–10 • Wool • 82 x 83 • Lancaster Co., Pennsylvania • Private collection • Made by Barbara Fisher.
Feather wreaths in the center and feather plume motifs characterize Lancaster Co. Amish quilts. The abundance
and quality of the quilting on this example would indicate that it is a comparatively early quilt.

Center Diamond

Circa 1910 • Wool • 82 x 82 • Lancaster Co.,
Pennsylvania • Private collection.
This quilt, made for Henry S. Fisher, is
initialed "H" on the back.

Center Diamond

Circa 1920 • Wool • 74 x 75 • Lancaster Co.,
Pennsylvania • M. Finkle and Daughter,
Philadelphia, PA.
Quilted baskets fill the outer border of this
quilt. The corner blocks contain a stylized
tulip. The tulip, along with several of the other
motifs, is double quilted, a practice often found
in early quilts but dropped in later years as
quilting became less full.

Center Diamond
Circa 1910 • Wool • 78 x 79 • Lancaster Co.,
Pennsylvania • Private collection • Made by
Rebecca Zook.
Although blocks are common on the borders
of Lancaster Co. quilts, this example has none.
Its intense colors and the simplicity of its pieced
design create a strong visual statement.

Center Diamond
Circa 1915 • Wool • 76 x 77 • Lancaster Co.,
Pennsylvania • Dr. and Mrs. Donald M. Herr.
This quilt was made for Amos Zook by his
mother Frances (Fannie) Diener Zook in
Mascot, Lancaster Co.

Center Diamond
Circa 1930 • Cotton • 81 x 83 • Lancaster Co., Pennsylvania • Privately owned.
Using cotton fabric for quilts was unusual among the Lancaster Co. Amish who commonly chose wool. These quilting motifs also vary from the norm. The feathers on the border create a series of oval shapes, rather than the traditional curved feather design. The back of the quilt is a pieced Bars pattern (also cotton), making it equally attractive on either side.

Sawtooth Diamond
Circa 1920 • Wool • 79 x 82 • Lancaster Co., Pennsylvania • Private collection.
Most Sawtooth Diamond quilts use only two colors: one for the sawtooth triangles and the other for the rest of the field. The quilter chose to use navy for the sawtooth border and the triangular pieces, giving this quilt an added dimension that would not have been achieved, had she followed the norm and used the red fabric in the triangles.

Center Diamond
Circa 1930 • Wool • 78 x 78 • Lancaster Co.,
Pennsylvania • Private collection.
Quilts of this pattern often have a series of
borders: one surrounding the center diamond,
one framing the square and then a wide outer
border. This quilter eliminated the first border
and let the diamond stand alone.

(below) Sawtooth Diamond
Circa 1920–30 • Wool • 85 x 86 • Lancaster Co.,
Pennsylvania • Dr. and Mrs. Donald M. Herr.
The sawtooth edge added a challenge in piecing this otherwise simple Center Diamond
pattern. This quilt deviates from the usual
practice of using a circular feather and star
quilting motif in the Center Diamond. Four
roses in full bloom fill the center of this
example.

Sunshine Diamond

Circa 1930 • Wool • 76 x 77 • Lancaster Co.,
Pennsylvania • Dr. and Mrs. Donald M. Herr.
The quilting motifs used here show some of
the changes in Lancaster Co. Amish quilts
from the turn of the century to 1940. The inner
border uses grapes and grape leaves, a design
frequently seen in earlier quilts. Their placement here, however, is much more widely
spaced and was done with only about half as
much quilting as on earlier examples. The
outer border uses a lovely but less time-
consuming rose motif, rather than the elaborate feather quilting seen often in earlier quilts.

Center Square

Circa 1890 • Wool • 75 x 78 • Lancaster Co.,
Pennsylvania • Privately owned.
The Center Square is an old pattern and
seems to be a forerunner to the more common
Center Diamond. The colors of this example
are soft, natural colors. In later years quiltmakers seemed to prefer a variety of bright jewel
tones.

Sunshine Diamond
Circa 1920–30 • Wool • 81 x 81 • Lancaster Co., Pennsylvania • Privately owned.
Two frequently used quilt patterns among the Lancaster County Amish were the Center Diamond and the Sunshine and Shadow. This quilt combines the two patterns into one. Most of the colors used are those of Amish clothing. There is one exception—the bright red, though used in quiltmaking, would not qualify as an appropriate choice for shirts or dresses according to Amish understanding.

Center Diamond
Circa 1920 • Wool • 81 x 82 • Lancaster Co.,
Pennsylvania • Norma J. Wangel.
The taupe color is unusually light for Lancaster County quilts of this period. The quilting motifs are typical feather plumes on the border with a rose and tulip spray on the triangular sections and feather wreaths in the center.

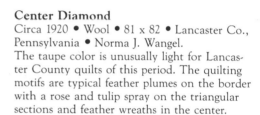

Center Diamond
Circa 1920 • Wool • 77 x 77 • Lancaster Co.,
Pennsylvania • Bryce and Donna Hamilton.
The corner blocks in the outer border of this quilt are filled with an overflowing bowl of fruit quilted in precise detail.

SUNSHINE AND SHADOW

Sunshine and Shadow
Circa 1925–30 • Wool • 84 x 86 • Lancaster Co., Pennsylvania • Dr. and Mrs. Donald M. Herr • Made by Sarah Beiler, Paradise, PA, for Rachel Beiler Lantz, born 1910.
The use of a pieced inner border adds interest to this quilt. Inner borders were common, but they were most often done as a solid strip of fabric.

Sunshine and Shadow
Circa 1930 • Wool • 75 x 76 • Lancaster Co., Pennsylvania • Dr. and Mrs. Donald M. Herr.
The rambling rose on this border was fast and easy to quilt, compared to the delicate feathers on the quilts of earlier years.

Sunshine and Shadow
Circa 1930 • Wool, cotton and rayon • 78 x 79 • Lancaster Co., Pennsylvania • Elizabeth Warren.
An inner border and corner blocks were commonly used by Lancaster Co. quiltmakers. Here the colors in the interior blocks are grouped in families from light to dark, creating diamond-shaped bands of color.

(below) **Sunshine and Shadow**
Circa 1910 • Wool • 80 x 83 • Lancaster Co., Pennsylvania • Private collection.
Fruit baskets with braided handles are quilted in this outer border. The corner blocks appear to have been filled at one time with a quilted feather wreath, although quilting in the corner blocks is now inexistent.

Sunshine and Shadow
Circa 1930 • Wool • Approx. 78 x 78 • Lancaster Co., Pennsylvania • America Hurrah, New York City.
The inner border of this quilt contains grapes and grape leaves, a design seen frequently on quilts from earlier decades. The outer border, however, is much more sparsely quilted and uses a floral motif seen frequently in the '30s and '40s.

Sunshine and Shadow
Circa 1930 • Cotton, wool and rayon • 79 x
79 • Lancaster Co., Pennsylvania • Private
collection.
The bright squares of this quilt are framed
within an equally bright pink inner border.
The blue border is filled with quilted baskets
and the entire quilt is contained within a
vibrantly colored binding.

Sunshine and Shadow
Circa 1930 • Cotton, wool and rayon • 79 x
79 • Lancaster Co., Pennsylvania • Catherine
Anthony.
This quilt shows the use of vivid colors in
sharp contrast to each other, a practice popular among Lancaster Co. Amish quilters in the
early 1900s.

Sunshine and Shadow
Circa 1930 • Wool, cotton and rayon • 82 x 82 • Lancaster Co., Pennsylvania • Bryce and Donna Hamilton.
The use of synthetic fabrics became quite popular among Amish women. Their availability and easy care made them
a favorite for clothing. Synthetics began to appear in quilts in the 1930s, as fine wool, so prevalent in early quilts,
became expensive and difficult to acquire.

BARS

Split Bars
Circa 1915 • Wool • 74 x 74 • Lancaster Co., Pennsylvania • Private collection.
This quilt is unusual in several ways. Its borders on the top, bottom and sides are of two different colors, while most quilts used the same color all around. Black strips on each side of the corner blocks seem to extend the inner border to the binding. Quilting motifs deviate from the frequently used feathers, grapes and diamonds and, instead, are a wide variety of unusual designs, both in the interior bars and the exterior border.

(above) Bars
Circa 1900 • Cotton • 71 x 78 • Lancaster
Co., Pennsylvania • Judi Boisson, Antique
American Quilts, New York City.
The use of cotton fabric in Amish quilts of
Lancaster Co., is the exception rather than the
norm. While cotton was used extensively in
nearby Mifflin Co., and in other Amish settle-
ments, Lancaster Co. quilters chose wool
almost exclusively before 1930.

Bars
Circa 1910 • Wool • 76 x 83 • Lancaster Co.,
Pennsylvania • Private collection • Made by
Rebecca Zook.
Piecing a quilt of this pattern was not difficult.
It seems that the quiltmaker compensated for
the lack of challenge in the piecework by doing
elaborate and extensive quilting. Evident in
this example is her careful attention to the
symmetry of design and precision in stitching.

Bars
Circa 1910 • Wool • 74 x 79 • Lancaster Co., Pennsylvania • Bettie Mintz, All of Us Americans Folk Art, Bethesda, MD.
The spaces between the large baskets on the border are filled with miniature versions of the same basket.

Split Bars
Circa 1920 • Wool • Approx. 74 x 76 • Lancaster Co., Pennsylvania • America Hurrah, New York City.
Here is evidence of the precise workmanship typical on quilts of this period. The geometric bars are softened with a double feather wreath and star in a central octagonal design.

Multiple Patch in Bars
Circa 1895 • Wool • 73 x 83 • Lancaster Co., Pennsylvania • Ida Kennel Winters.
This quilt was presumably made by Emma Fisher and her sisters for Emma's hope chest when Emma was about 18 years old. She was married to John T. Byler, December 21, 1899. Emma was born December 9, 1877 and died October 10, 1939.

Bars
Circa 1930 • Wool • 86 x 92 • Lancaster Co., Pennsylvania • Dr. and Mrs. Donald M. Herr.
Many Bars quilts were made with the intention that the pattern should run vertically on the bed. The proportions of this quilt would indicate that the bars were to lie horizontally on the bed.

Bars

Circa 1940 • Wool • 80 x 84 • Lancaster Co.,
Pennsylvania • Catherine Anthony.
Here are simple, basic design elements, yet the
rich colors in combination with each other
make a dramatic statement.

(below right) **Bars**

Circa 1900 • Wool • 66 x 82 • Lancaster Co.,
Pennsylvania • Bettie Mintz, All of Us Americans Folk Art, Bethesda, MD.
Although unusual for Bars quilts, this one has
grape vines quilted on the alternate gray bars.
Additionally, the side borders are wider than
the upper and lower borders, and a rope quilting motif has been added to fill in the open
space.

Bars

Circa 1930 • Wool • Approx. 80 x 81 • Lancaster Co., Pennsylvania • America Hurrah, New York City.
Two strong colors and the use of a carefully executed inner border make this simple Lancaster Co., PA pattern a
stunning quilt.

CHINESE COINS

Blocks and Bars
Circa 1910 • Wool • 82 x 80 • Mifflin Co.,
Pennsylvania • America Hurrah, New York
City.
This is likely a variation of the Bars pattern so
commonly used by the Amish of nearby
Lancaster Co. This quilt's proportionately
more narrow borders, narrower binding and
varied colors on the binding are indications of
the quilt's Mifflin Co. heritage.

(below right) **Chinese Coins**
Circa 1940 • Cotton • 73 x 86 • Ohio
• M. Finkle and Daughter, Philadelphia, PA.
Lighter, pastel colors became more prominent
in Ohio quilts after 1930. During the transition, lighter colors were often used in conjunc-
tion with darker, more conservative shades, as
shown here.

Chinese Coins
Circa 1940 • Cotton • Approx. 73 x 83 • Ohio • America Hurrah, New York City.
Although similar in design to the Bars pattern commonly found in Lancaster, PA, Chinese Coins was a pattern
frequently used by Amish women of the Midwest.

Chinese Coins
Circa 1925 • Cotton • 69 x 79 • Private collection.
This quiltmaker was intrigued with the Chinese Coins pattern. She used it not only in the center, but continued the theme in the inner border, breaking it into diagonals at the intersecting corner blocks. This pattern lends itself well to using fabric scraps leftover from other sewing projects.

DISTINCTIVE FEATURES OF AMISH QUILTS

	SHAPE	BORDERS	BINDINGS	FABRICS
Lancaster County, PA	Quilts are generally square, measuring between 70–84 inches square.	Borders are distinctively wide, often measuring from 10–15 inches in width. Corner blocks are frequently used and are proportionately large to match border width. Borders are most often solid strips of fabric without additional piecework.	Bindings are distinctively wide, measuring from 1–2 inches. Binding is usually a separate fabric sewn by machine to the top of the quilt and then wrapped around and stitched either by hand or by machine.	Fabric choices are almost always fine wools for quilt top. Cottons may be used on backings.
Mifflin County, PA	Quilts are generally rectangular in shape with length being approximately 10 inches longer than width.	Borders are generally from 4–8 inches wide. Corner blocks are less common than in Lancaster quilts and are proportionately smaller to match border width.	Early bindings are ½–¾ inch wide; occasionally wider. Some bindings are sewn, or edges are finished by wrapping extra backing fabric over the raw edges to the quilt top or from the quilt top to the back. Bindings may consist of several different fabrics along a single edge, in keeping with the "scrap" quilt tradition of Mifflin Co. quiltmakers. Less conservative groups sometimes did fancy or scalloped bindings.	Early quilts (c. 1900) used some wools, sometimes combined with cottons in the same quilt top. Later quilts were predominately cotton. Rayon appeared as early as 1920s due likely to the establishment of a rayon manufacturing plant in nearby Lewistown.
Ohio	Quilts are generally rectangular in shape.	Borders are generally 4–8 inches wide. Inner borders are found on majority of Ohio quilts; both inner and outer borders may be enhanced with piecework. Piecework on borders includes zigzags, blocks, Chinese Coins, sawtooth and piano key (a sequence of light and dark rectangles).	Bindings are generally from ¼–1 inch wide. Bindings sometimes wrapped from backing to front and sometimes were sewn on as a separate piece. Bindings often matched the inner border. Early examples often have rounded corners. Appliqued and fancy bindings are seen from the mid-1920s. Scalloped edges became very popular about 1940.	Sateens, chambray and plain weave cotton were preferred. Wools were used in some early quilts but cotton was dominant.
Indiana	Quilts are generally rectangular in shape.	Borders are generally 4–8 inches wide. Inner borders are found on most examples. Corner blocks are uncommon. Borders are usually plain. Fewer examples of pieced borders than on Ohio quilts.	Bindings are very similar to Ohio quilts. Few examples of fancy bindings or scalloped edges.	Wool was used in some early quilts but cotton was the dominant choice.
Arthur, Illinois	Quilts show a wide variety in pattern and color. Fabrics are often wools rather than cottons, as in other midwestern quilts of the period. Colors tend to be rich, dark colors including greens, plums and reds. Patterns are often abstract designs. Piecework is more random and graphic. Arthur quilts seem to exhibit the discipline of Amish quiltmaking without rigidity.			

The chart below compares distinguishing features of antique Amish quilts made in the oldest Amish communities in North America between 1890 and 1940. There are presently established Old Order communities in 21 states and one Canadian province. The settlements dating from the late 1800s are located in Pennsylvania, Ohio, Indiana, Illinois, Iowa, Kansas and Ontario, Canada. From these, the largest number of collected quilts have come from Pennsylvania, Ohio, Indiana and Illinois. Quilts made during the first half of the twentieth century in these areas have characteristics that can generally identify them as being from a particular region.

When summarizing such a large body of material one is obviously forced to make generalizations. There are always exceptions. This overview looks at the broad strokes and makes general observations and comparisons. We are grateful for the contributions of quilt collectors across the country who helped by way of conversations, questionnaires and writings.

BACKINGS	PATTERNS	QUILTING	COLORS	WORKMANSHIP
Quilt backings exhibit great variety of fabrics including plain and patterned weave fabrics. Solid colored cotton, cotton flannel and cotton chambray are common. It is not unusual to find printed fabrics used as backing fabric in this community.	Center Diamond, Bars and Sunshine and Shadow patterns are almost exclusively from Lancaster Co. Other popular patterns include Baskets, Irish Chain, Double Nine-Patch, Crazy, Lone Star and Log Cabin.	Quilting is extensive and elaborate. Common quilting motifs include feathers, baskets, stars, fiddlehead ferns, tulips and roses, grapes and grapeleaves, pumpkin seeds. Simple diamonds or squares may be used to fill in open areas. Earlier quilts often have double stitched quilting lines.	Early quilts (before 1900) exhibit more muted colors including browns, greens, grays and medium to darker blues and reds. After 1900 the colors become much brighter and include jewel tones of purples, royal blues, brighter greens, wine. Black is used only rarely and not used as a main color.	Expert craftsmanship is shown in both piece-work and quilting. A great deal of attention is given to every detail of the quilt.
Backings usually consist of solid colored cotton fabrics.	Patterns were almost always done in blocks separated with sashing. Most patterns are some variation of the basic Four-Patch or Nine-Patch design. There are a few examples of Bars or Sunshine and Shadow patterns but their proportions are rectangular rather than square as in Lancaster examples. Other patterns include Log Cabin, Jacob's Ladder, Crazy and Irish Chain.	Quilting motifs are much less ornate than on Lancaster quilts. Common motifs are simple cables, tulips, hearts, blackberry leaf and other leaf designs, and single chains.	Colors vary depending on how conservative the quiltmaker's church district was. The conservative Nebraska Amish used predominately blues, browns and purples. Less conservative groups (Byler and Peachy churches) used bright colors, including hot pinks, bright blues, yellows, greens, purples and oranges in combination with each other or with shades of blue, brown or black. Mifflin County quilts are usually scrap quilts and, even when employing only 3 or 4 colors, often used several shades of each color to complete the quilt top.	Overall workmanship in both quilting and piecework was less precise than in neighboring Lancaster County. Mifflin Co. quilters seemed to take a more frugal, practical approach to quiltmaking.
Quilt backs are almost always solid colored cottons.	A multitude of patterns were used. Most are repeated block designs, often with a plain block alternating with the pieced block. Railroad Crossing pattern seems unique to Ohio Amish. Other popular designs are Roman Stripe, Monkey Wrench, Log Cabin, Tumbling Blocks, Stars, Chinese Coins, Ocean Waves.	Quilting usually outlines pieced design or runs in straight lines across pieced patches. Plain blocks often have feather wreath or another independent quilted design. Border quilting motifs include cables, twisted rope, fiddlehead fern and some feathers.	Early quilts use browns, blues and greens. After 1900 black began being used as a main background color. Two-color quilts were common. Color range grew to include nearly every color under the rainbow. Pastel shades began to replace the brighter colors about 1930.	Ohio quiltmakers seem to prefer piecework to quilting. Great attention is given to accurate and precise piecework. Quilting, though often good quality, is generally less abundant and lavish than on Lancaster quilts.
Solid colored cottons were used for backings.	Large variety of patterns were used. Many repeated block patterns. Indiana quilters were more likely to set pieced blocks against each other to create a secondary pattern, rather than set pieced blocks against plain blocks. Popular patterns include Fan, Streak of Lightning, Ocean Waves, Shoo-fly, Monkey Wrench and Log Cabin. Indiana Log Cabins often used 2 little squares in the center of the Log Cabin patch, giving the quilt a unique look.	Pieced blocks were often quilted in double or triple straight lines. Plain blocks often have a quilted feather wreath or floral motif. Outer borders often have angled straight lines, cables or fans.	Colors are similar to Ohio quilts. Fewer examples of 2-color quilts and fewer quilts with black as the dominant color. Quilts use a wide variety of colors.	Size and scale of piece-work and quilting seem larger and somewhat less precise than Ohio quilts. Indiana quilts seem less bound by convention than quilts from other larger Amish communities.

MULTIPLE PATCH

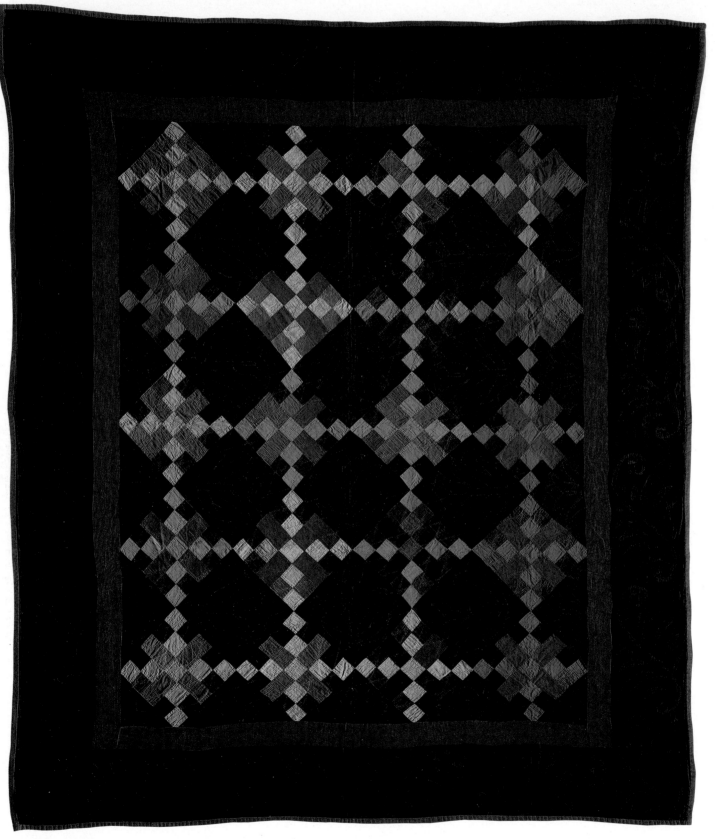

Four-Patch
Circa 1930 • Cotton • Approx. 70 x 81 • Ohio • Rosallene Barrett Bradshaw.
The construction and placement of the colors in this quilt make it look like a Single Irish Chain. A fiddlehead fern motif is quilted in the outer border and the plain black squares hold a quilted tulip.

Four-Patch
1903 • Wool and cotton • 62 x 82 • Holmes
Co., Ohio • Private collection • Made by Mrs.
Albert M. Yoder.
Even though this is a scrap quilt it is obvious
that the quiltmaker planned the placement of
the colors. The center row of patches and the
vertical rows on either side of it are basically
the same throughout. The addition of the
Chinese Coins inner border unifies the whole.

Four-Patch and Blockwork • Circa 1920 •
Cotton • Approx. 60 x 84 • Mifflin Co.,
Pennsylvania • America Hurrah, New
York City.
This Four-Patch pattern has a distinctive look
because of the way in which its colors are
placed. The purple blocks around the perime-
ter of the pieced blocks create the feeling of an
inner border.

Nine-Patch in Blockwork
Circa 1930 • Cotton • 69 x 80 • Indiana
The sashing around the simple Nine-Patch
block creates a distinctive version of this
pattern.

Sixteen-Patch
Circa 1930 • Cotton • 70 x 81 • Mifflin Co.,
Pennsylvania • Bettie Mintz, All of Us
Americans Folk Art, Bethesda, MD.
This quilt belonged to the Yoder family; the
initials "H.Y." and "A.Y." are embroidered
in one corner. The combination of blue and
brown fabrics suggests that the origins of this
quilt are likely Mifflin County.

Nine-Patch in Blockwork
Circa 1910–20 • Cotton • 70 x 80 • Mifflin Co., Pennsylvania • William and Connie Hayes.
Quilting seemed of less importance to quilters of Mifflin Co., as compared to Lancaster Co., Pennsylvania. Mifflin
Co. quilting designs are, in general, larger in scale, less difficult and less ornate.

Double Nine-Patch
Circa 1930 • Wool • Approx. 80 x 80 • Lancaster Co., Pennsylvania • America Hurrah, New York City.
In contrast to the Nine-Patch quilts of neighboring Mifflin Co., Pennsylvania, the Lancaster Co. examples have wider borders, wider bindings and much less use of the color brown. The fabrics used are predominantly wool rather than cotton, and Lancaster Co. quilts are likely to have much more elaborate and decorative quilting motifs.

Nine-Patch • Circa 1935 • Wool • 86 x 86 •
Lancaster Co., Pennsylvania • Norma
J. Wangel.
The Nine-Patch quilts made by Amish quilters
in Lancaster County were seldom done with
sashing. Usually each Nine-Patch block was set
against a plain-colored block of equal size. In
contrast, the individual blocks of Mifflin Co.
quilts are most often surrounded by sashing or
strips of fabric which frame the pieced blocks
and form grids between them.

(*below right*) **Nine-Patch**
Circa 1930 • Cotton • 74 x 86 • Mifflin Co.,
Pennsylvania • Bill Kulczycki.
The dull colors used in this quilt are typical of
the more conservative Amish communities of
Mifflin Co. Their colors and quilting designs
portray a more austere approach toward
quiltmaking.

(*above*) **Nine-Patch**
Circa 1930 • Cotton • 75 x 81 • Ohio • Judi Boisson, Antique American Quilts, New York City.
The small pieces and variety of fabrics in this example seem to indicate that it was a scrap quilt. When the quilter
used the last remnants of one piece of fabric, she simply moved on to the next.

Blockwork

Circa 1935 • Cotton • 75 x 84 • Mifflin Co.,
Pennsylvania • William and Connie Hayes •
Made by Fanny Byler.

At first glance this quilt appears to be made of
only three different colors. Upon closer examination, it is obvious that there are at least two
shades of purple and three or more shades of
blue. Their interplay, though it appears to be
accidental rather than planned, adds energy
to the quilt.

Double Nine-Patch

Circa 1930 • Wool and cotton • 74 x 81 •
Mifflin Co., Pennsylvania • William and
Connie Hayes.

Typically the quilts of the Nebraska Amish
group of Mifflin Co., use very subdued colors,
most often only purples, blues and browns.
The patterns are usually a four-patch or nine-
patch variation. Because of the strict religious
guidelines of this conservative group, it is relatively simple to identify quilts made by the
Nebraska Amish. This quilt was made for
Jacob B. Hostetler and bears his initials.

Double Nine-Patch
Circa 1930 • Wool • Approx. 80 x 80 • Lancaster Co., Pennsylvania • America Hurrah, New York City.
The careful placement of purple in the center of the Nine-Patch blocks makes a large X across the interior of this quilt. Feather wreaths, their centers covered with tiny quilted squares, fill the large purple block. The border is decorated with feather quilting.

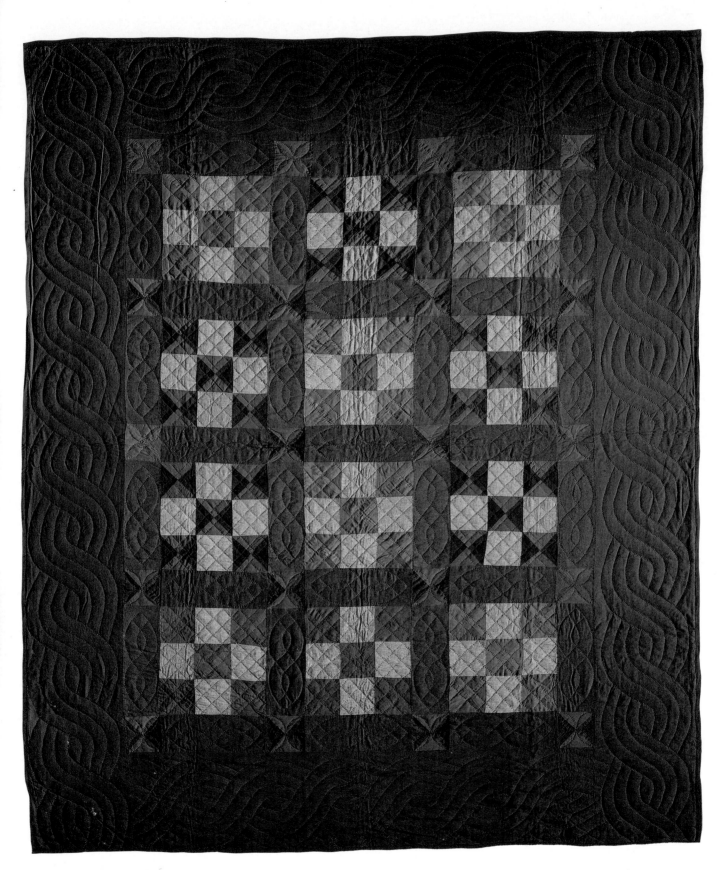

Triangle Nine-Patch
Circa 1935 • Cotton and rayon • 71 x 84 • Mifflin Co., Pennsylvania • Jill and Henry Barber.
The practice of embroidering initials on quilts was common among the Nebraska Amish of Mifflin Co. This example is initialed "R.L.H."

Four-Patch

Circa 1930 • Cotton • 66 x 66 • Mifflin Co., Pennsylvania • Jill and Henry Barber. Quilters of Mifflin Co. seem to have taken a frugal, practical approach to quiltmaking. Quilts often seem to have been made from a collection of leftover fabrics rather than having been a pre-planned unit. In this example, all but three of the Four-Patch units are alike. Perhaps the quiltmaker used all the mustard-colored fabric and filled in with whatever was on hand.

Nine-Patch

Circa 1940 • Cotton • 85 x 85 • Lancaster Co., Pennsylvania • Norma J. Wangel. This simple Nine-Patch shows some of the changes in later quiltmaking in Lancaster Co. The fabric is cotton rather than wool. The lines quilted diagonally in the interior of the quilt are spaced further apart than on earlier examples. The outer border, rather than being quilted fully in an intricate feather design, has more open space and is a more easily quilted floral motif.

Double Nine-Patch
Circa 1928 • Cotton • 70 x 90 • Indiana •
Bryce and Donna Hamilton.
This quilt is initialed "M.N." and dated
"February 24, 1928." An unusual scroll and
half-moon design are quilted in the border
of this example.

Single Irish Chain or Double Nine-Patch
Circa 1930 • Cotton • 76 x 90 • Missouri •
Catherine Anthony.
Construction of the Double Nine-Patch and
Single Irish Chain is identical. To create the
chain, the Nine-Patch blocks are done in two
colors placed in relation to each other so that
one color forms an unbroken line both vertically and horizontally. The plain patches of
this quilt are beautifully quilted with a circular
feather. The border quilting is in double diagonal lines.

Double Irish Chain
Circa 1910 • Cotton • 74 x 83 • Ohio • Private collection.
Sharp contrast in color makes this a strong graphic design. When done in a shape other than square, the Irish Chain piecework ends differently at top and bottom, as shown in this example.

Double Irish Chain
1894 • Wool • 84 x 84 • Lancaster Co., Pennsylvania • Bettie Mintz, All of Us Americans Folk Art, Bethesda, MD.
The date "1894" and initials "K.B." and "S.B." are beautifully quilted in the lower center patch of this quilt.

Triple Irish Chain

Circa 1930 • Cotton and wool • 83 x 81 •
Pennsylvania • Jill and Henry Barber.
The shape, wide border and pattern of this
quilt all suggest a strong Lancaster County
influence. However, its narrow binding and
sparse quilting designs seem to indicate that its
origins are somewhere outside of Lancaster
County.

Triple Irish Chain

Circa 1905 • Cotton • 80 x 80 • Somerset
Co., Pennsylvania • Gregory M. McCauley.
The quilts of Somerset County generally show
the combined influence of Lancaster and
midwestern Amish communities. This example
has a wide binding and square shape typical
of Lancaster quilts, but its simple quilting designs
and multiple border treatment are more typical
of midwestern quilts. The use of yellow
reflects the influence of communities outside
Lancaster.

Double Irish Chain
Circa 1930 • Cotton • 70 x 70 • Ohio •
Nonie Fisher.
Two light colors stand out sharply against the
black background. The double inner border
enhances and completes the piecework.

Double Irish Chain
Circa 1930 • Cotton • 74 x 91 • Ohio • Bryce
and Donna Hamilton.
Many quilts from Ohio were pieced on black
backgrounds. Here the choice of black provides
contrast and gives energy to the pieced design.

Log Cabin
Circa 1910 .• Wool • 70 x 71 • Lancaster Co., Pennsylvania • Mr. and Mrs. Mel Lapp.
Log Cabin quilts were often not quilted. In some cases the layers were held together by tying threads at regular intervals across the surface of the quilt top. In other cases, as in this example, the layers were connected only by the binding at the outer edge.

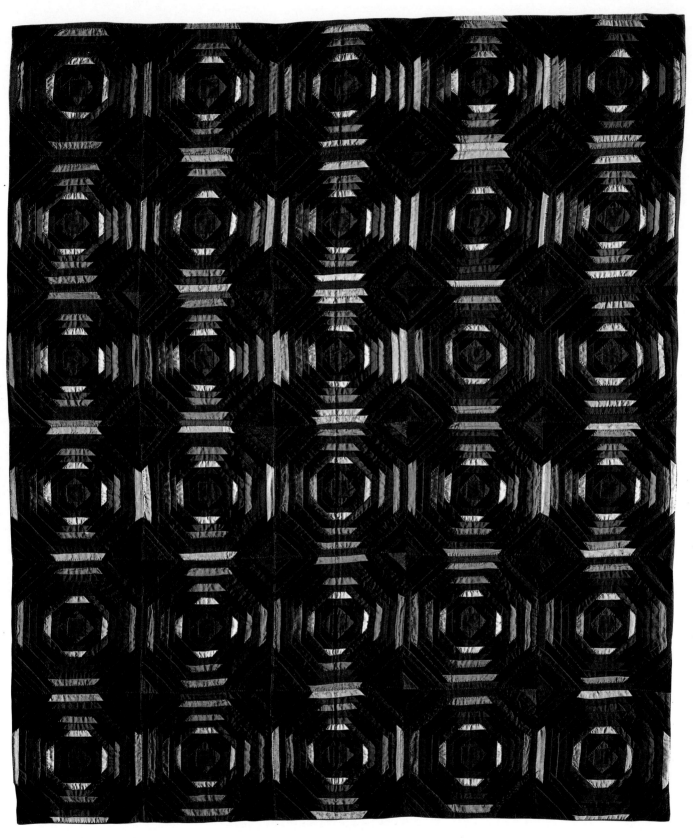

Pineapple Log Cabin
Circa 1940 • Wool and cotton • 63 x 77 • Kitchener, Ontario • Private collection.
The "Pineapple" arrangement is one of the many variations of the Log Cabin quilt pattern. Many Log Cabin quilts were left unquilted, especially if they were made with heavier fabrics. Because they were pieced in narrow strips, the seam allowances underneath were close together and bulky, making quilting extremely difficult. This one, however, is quilted in every other pieced row.

50

Log Cabin
Circa 1930 • Cotton • 66 x 80 • Indiana •
Judi Boisson, Antique American Quilts,
New York City.
Log Cabin quilts from Indiana are often distin-
guished by the varying shapes and sizes of
their patches, giving the quilts a more random
and individually unique appearance.

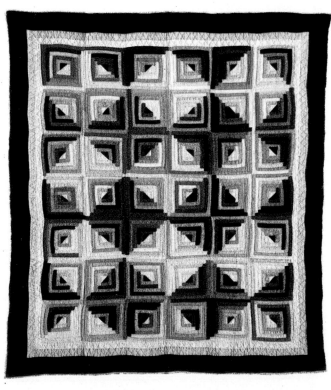

Log Cabin
Circa 1935 • Cotton • 67 x 76 • Ohio
In the late 1930s and early '40s, pastel colors
began to be used in quiltmaking. The changes
happened gradually, with darker colors remain-
ing prominent, while used in combination with
a variety of lighter fabrics.

Log Cabin
Circa 1900 • Wool • 77 x 90 • Mifflin Co.,
Pennsylvania • William and Connie Hayes,
Darwin D. Bearley.
Made by Rachel Bawell, wife of Samuel J.
Peight, this quilt was given to their son Daniel
B., and then to his son John J.

(below) **Log Cabin**
Circa 1920 • Wool • 64 x 74 • Wisconsin •
Bryce and Donna Hamilton.
Although she used a large variety of fabrics,
this quiltmaker successfully pieced the blocks,
using light colors on one side and dark colors
on the other, to create a zigzag design.

Log Cabin
Circa 1910–15 • Wool and cotton • 64 x 70 • Mifflin Co., Pennsylvania • Jill and Henry Barber.
The Log Cabin pattern has a multitude of design possibilities, depending upon the assembly of its pieced blocks.
This particular design is called "Barnraising."

Log Cabin
Circa 1920 • Wool and cotton • 62 x 75 • Mifflin Co., Pennsylvania • Judi Boisson, Antique American Quilts, New York City.
This quilt is initialed "F.M." Its colorful piecework extends to a randomly pieced border along the upper and lower edges. The quiltmaker's placement of the Log Cabin blocks created a "Straight Furrows" design.

FROM BEDROOM TO OFFICE

In a highly technical society, filled with machines, talking computers and identity by number, many people are drawn to handcrafted works of art. There is comfort in the knowledge that the creative spirit survives.

Antique Amish quilts are collected today, primarily for display as art objects, rather than as bedcovers. Their bold geometric shapes, their rich colors and soft natural fiber fabrics add warmth to any environment. Examples of fine Amish quilts hang in executive offices of major corporations throughout the world. They have been compared to modern art paintings and are acclaimed by art critics. They command prices comparable to works of accomplished artists.

Ironically, these quilts come from a community that places little value on art. Within the Old Order Amish mentality, the creation of an object solely on the basis of aesthetics is believed to be poor use of one's time and talents. The Old Order Amish do appreciate beauty, especially if it is in some way combined with function. A beautifully painted blanket chest, a carefully executed quilt, elaborately embroidered pillow cases and a hand-painted family record all serve utilitarian purposes, while also being creative expressions. The many fine examples of Amish decorative arts would seem to indicate that the group's discipline has focused the energies of its members, rather than stifling their creative spirits. Perhaps working within limitations has been an inspiration rather than a deterrent.

The best antique Amish quilts served not only a function but also served the soul. Some of these old quilts appear to have never been used. According to their oral histories, many of them were made to commemorate the marriage of a son or daughter. A quilt of this type was likely stored in a chest and placed on the bed only for special times when company was coming. It could then be viewed, admired and put away again. Was this valuing a quilt primarily for its aesthetic value? The Amish quiltmaker knew that her masterpiece *could* and *would* be used for warmth if needed!

Quilts served another purpose as well. Women sat together at the quilt frame, likely sharing their frustrations and joys. It is difficult to say whether a quilting is

Family wash frolics in a summer breeze.

(Above) Serenity fills the countryside and the people who live there.
(Below) The chance of this person becoming a quilter would be greater if he were a girl.

work or pleasure. In the Amish community it is both. In years gone by quilting usually included a gathering of mother, daughters, sisters, aunts, grandmothers and friends who spent the day quilting (the actual process of stitching together in a decorative pattern three layers of the quilt). These women shared similar life experiences and values. Around the quilt frame they produced a quilt, but they also reinforced the values and support systems of the Amish way of life. What happened in the past continues today. Information and expectations are passed across the generations at the day-long outings. Children playing around the quilt frame overhear the conversation and absorb it. Younger girls beginning to quilt also learn what is expected of them as grown Amish women.

When one views Amish quilts strictly as art objects, they are only beautiful. When one understands the community from which the quilts come, they become more than striking art pieces. Quilts communicate some of the wholeness of life. They have become treasures, not only for the beauty of their design, but also for the values of faith, solidity and commitment that they symbolize in a world that too often seems fragmented and too busy to care.

Broken Star
Circa 1930 • Cotton • 76 x 81 • Ohio • Private collection.
This example demonstrates this Amish woman's love and appreciation for beautiful things. Her creative energy was not wasted. The workmanship is impeccable from the pieced design, to the quilting, to the appliqued sawtooth binding.

Broken Star
1938 • Cotton • 77 x 77 • Mt. Hope, Holmes,
Co., Ohio • Catherine Anthony.
This quilt was made by Katie Miller Kurtz
for her daughter Rebecca Kurtz Hershberger at
the time of her marriage in 1938. The quilt
shows its maker's skill in both piecing and
quilting.

Lone Star
1938 • Wool and cotton • 87 x 89 • Lancaster
Co., Pennsylvania • Dr. and Mrs. Donald
M. Herr.
This colorful Star appears to be floating in a
sky of purple. A winding rose quilting motif
decorates the border; feathers and crosshatch-
ing fill the square and triangular blocks around
the Star.

Lone Star
Circa 1931 • Cotton • 84 x 84 • Indiana •
Barbara S. Janos.
Golden yellow, a color avoided by Amish
quilters in Lancaster County, was used by
quiltmakers in the Amish communities in the
Midwest.

Lone Star
1927 • Cotton • 74 x 78 • Ohio •
Diana Leone.
This quilt is initialed "J.H." and dated "Jan-
uary 11, 1927." The fabrics are arranged in a
"reverse repeat" pattern, in which the color
sequence starts in the center, goes out to the
widest part of the star and then repeats the
sequence in reverse. The band of black on
either side of the beige color makes the star
seem to pulsate.

Variable Star

1905 • Wool • Approx. 63 x 77 • Ohio • America Hurrah, New York City.

This early Ohio example is made from wool, although cotton was the main choice of fabric for Ohio quiltmaking. This quilter obviously enjoyed piecework. After piecing all the Stars in this pattern, she topped it off with a pieced inner border, creating a stunning overall look.

Strip Star
Circa 1950 • Cotton • 66 x 77 • Ohio • Judi Boisson, Antique American Quilts, New York City.
This quilt demonstrates the precise piecework done by most Ohio quiltmakers. Set against a typical black field, the Stars seem to dance.

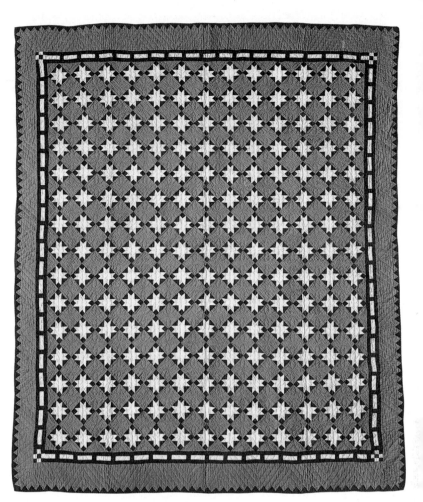

195 Stars
Circa 1910 • Cotton sateen • 68 x 83 •
Holmes Co., Ohio • Private collection.
Ohio quiltmakers seemed to give precedence to
the piecing of a quilt rather than the quilting
stitches. This example shows that priority, not
only in its many small Stars, but also in its
pieced inner border and appliqued sawtooth
binding.

Variable Star
Circa 1925 • Cotton • 62 x 89 • Ohio • Bryce
and Donna Hamilton.
Two-color quilts were common among Ohio
quiltmakers; pieced blocks were set against
contrasting backgrounds. Here fine feather
quilting fills the alternate solid color blocks;
the pieced Stars are quilted with triple straight
lines.

Evening Star
Circa 1905 • Wool and cotton • 68 x 76 •
Indiana • Kathleen McGrady.
Made by the Gingerich family, this quilt was
likely made in Indiana and then traveled with
the family when they resettled in Missouri.

Pinwheel Star
Circa 1930 • Cotton • 74 x 87 • Ohio •
Catherine Anthony.
Quilts from Amish communities in the
Midwest frequently exhibit greater frugality
on the parts of their makers than do their
counterparts in Lancaster communities. This is
likely due largely to the fact that migrations
and resettling created economic stresses. This
quilt seems to have been made with leftover
fabrics. The black background is made with
several different fabrics; the pieced stars show
the substitution of several fabrics.

Stars

Circa 1930 • Cotton • 76 x 86 • Mifflin Co., Pennsylvania

This is a quilt made in one of the less conservative groups of Mifflin County. Most quilts from this area were based on the Four-Patch on Nine-Patch format. This is obviously a deviation from that norm. The grape quilting motif on the side borders is often seen on a smaller scale on quilts from nearby Lancaster Co., Pennsylvania.

Carpenter's Wheel
1939 • Cotton • 72 x 90 • Ohio • America Hurrah, New York City.
The quilter who invested the hours in this quilt signed it by quilting "E.Y." and "Feb. 8, 1939." She pieced not only the black background blocks but added pieced stars at the intersections of the sashing.

Variable Star
Circa 1910 • Cotton sateen and wool • 67 x 81 • Holmes Co., Ohio • Private collection • Made by Lucy L. Yoder.
Often it is the dominant design in a quilt that is given the brightest color. Here the quilt-maker used bright colors for the background sections of the pieced blocks, but black sateen for the solid color blocks and Stars.

Tumbling Blocks
Circa 1930 • Cotton • 67 x 83 • Ohio • The People's Place Quilt Museum, Intercourse, Pennsylvania.
By carefully placing the colors, the quiltmaker could effectively create the illusion of stacked cubes. Here a double inner border frames the Blocks and gives them stability.

Tumbling Blocks
Circa 1930 • Cotton • 75 x 88 • Ohio • Judi Boisson, Antique American Quilts, New York City.
The outer border of this quilt is covered with graceful fiddlehead ferns. There is an inner border, but its color is so similar to the outer border that it is difficult to distinguish.

Tumbling Blocks
Circa 1930 • Cotton and wool • 67 x 79 •
Ohio • Judi Boisson, Antique American
Quilts, New York City.
A sawtooth binding adds a special touch to
this quilt. Although its colors are random, the
quilt was the product of a quiltmaker with a
skilled eye who was able to achieve the stacked
cube effect.

(below right) **Tumbling Blocks**
Circa 1930-40 • Cotton • 70 x 79 • Southern
Wisconsin • Cyndi Davis.
This full-size quilt has a companion crib quilt
done in the same fabrics.

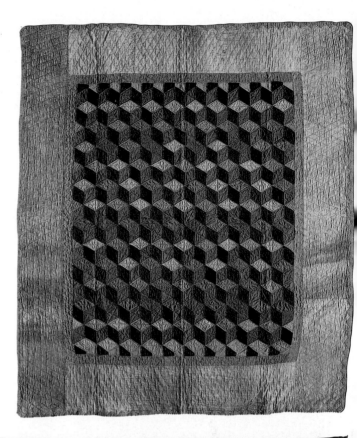

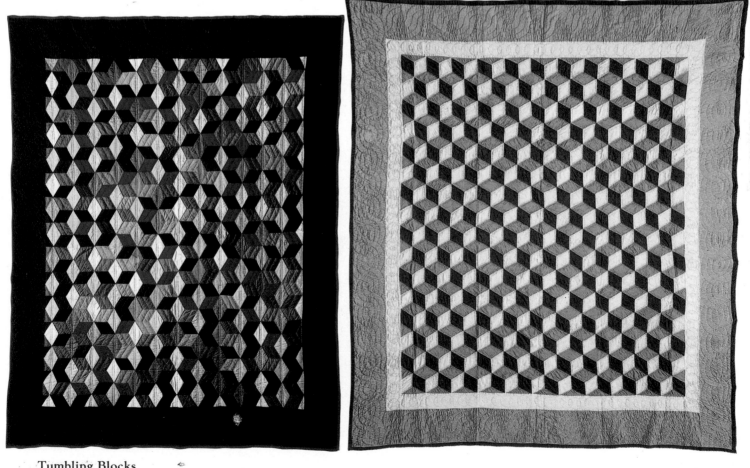

Tumbling Blocks
Circa 1920-30 • Cotton • Approx. 68 x 88 • Ohio • America Hurrah, New York City.
The random color placement in this quilt confuses the eye. At times, cubes dominate; at other times one sees
six-pointed stars; sometimes jagged vertical lines stand out.

OCEAN WAVES

Ocean Waves
Circa 1930 • Cotton • 74 x 79 • Holmes Co., Ohio • Catherine Anthony • Made by Katy Miller.
The blue green color of the background fabric seems a perfect choice for the Ocean Waves design.

Ocean Waves
Circa 1935-40 • Cotton • 70 x 82 • Ohio •
Judi Boisson, Antique American Quilts, New
York City.
Lighter colors and the use of a more showy
scalloped binding are signs of the transition
away from distinctive darker quilts to a more
modern, popular look.

Ocean Waves
Circa 1930 • Cotton • 69 x 79 • Ohio • Judi
Boisson, Antique American Quilts, New York
City.
This quiltmaker chose to use a double inner
border—one, the same purple as the back-
ground color, and the second, a sunny yellow.
The purple inner border sets the pieced trian-
gles apart and makes them appear to float in
the interior space.

(above left) **Ocean Waves**
Circa 1930 • Cotton • Approx. 79 x 79 •
Ohio • America Hurrah, New York City.
Sawtooth borders are most frequently done
using only two colors. The random colors in
the sawtooth inner border of this example are
in keeping with the apparently unplanned
placement of colors in the interior of the
design. Though random, the colors are well
balanced and set pleasingly within their black
field.

(above right) **Ocean Waves**
Circa 1926 • Cotton • 76 x 80 • Dover,
Delaware • Barbara S. Janos • Made by
Esther Schwartzentruber.
The red inner border highlights the little bit of
red used in the triangles. Beautiful fiddlehead
ferns are quilted in the outer border.

(left) **Ocean Waves**
1924 • Cotton sateen • 76 x 84 • Holmes Co.,
Ohio • Barbara S. Janos.
An orderly quilt, this one includes only two
colors per section, but then varies those colors
throughout the quilt. The quilting is in simple
straight lines—squares in the inner blocks and
diagonal lines on the border.

Ocean Waves
Circa 1920–30 • Cotton • 74 x 75 • Ohio • Bryce and Donna Hamilton.
It seems this quiltmaker was looking for a challenge. The open spaces of the Ocean Wave design are filled with pieced eight-pointed stars and the whole is contained within a Chinese Coins inner border.

CRAZY QUILTS

Crazy Quilt
Circa 1930 • Wool and cotton • 67 x 81 • Ontario, Canada • Privately owned.
It is difficult to know whether this should be called a Lone Star or a Crazy quilt. It is certainly a successful blending of the two designs.

Crazy Quilt
Circa 1910–20 • Wool and cotton • 69 x 78 •
Poole, Ontario, Canada • Privately owned.
This quilt was made in Canada prior to 1920
and was brought by the bride and groom to
Lancaster Co. when the newlyweds made their
home there.

Crazy Quilt
1939 • Wool • 62 x 73 • Lancaster Co., Pennsylvania • Kathryn and Dan McCauley.
Although this quilt started in the center as a
Crazy quilt, it became more symmetrical as it
expanded, ending in an orderly series of patchwork blocks.

Crazy Quilt
1928 • Wool • 88 x 89 • Lancaster Co., Pennsylvania • Private collection.
The quiltmaker initialed and dated her quilt on one block—"M.K. 1928." Crazy quilt blocks provided an opportunity to exhibit one's entire embroidery stitch repertoire.

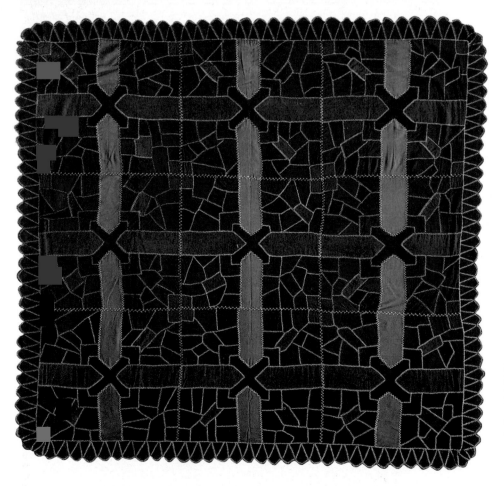

Crazy Quilt
Circa 1880 • Wool • 70 x 73 • Lancaster Co., Pennsylvania • Kathryn and Dan McCauley. This unusual Crazy quilt is certainly more daring than most Lancaster Co. examples. The sashing, purple X's, and cone border all set it apart as a one-of-a-kind example.

Crazy Quilt
1933 • Wool • 77 x 79 • Lancaster Co., Pennsylvania • Dr. and Mrs. Donald M. Herr.
The date "1933" and initials "S.S." are included in the fanciful embroidery stitches in the Crazy patch blocks. Like most Lancaster Co. Crazy quilts, this one sets the Crazy patch blocks alternately with plain quilted blocks, giving even the Crazy quilt a strong sense of order.

ABOUT THE AMISH

The Amish are first of all a Christian group. They believe the Bible is God's instruction manual for living. From the Amish point of view, if persons take the Holy Scripture seriously as a guide for living, their lives will be different from the majority of society. The Amish *are* dramatically different from the prevailing North American culture. Their distinctives are not practiced for the sake of being different, but are the result of the Amish church's attempt to live faithfully to God's teachings.

The Amish trace their roots to the 1500s. They are part of the radical left wing of the Protestant Reformation known as Anabaptism. This nickname resulted from their theology and practice of adult, voluntary baptism. Today, as then, they believe baptism is a symbol of one's willingness to align oneself with the life and teachings of Jesus Christ. Their effort to follow Christ, in all aspects of life has resulted in misunderstandings and differences with those for whom it is not a goal or priority.

Historically, the Anabaptists suffered persecution and martyrdom from Protestants and Catholics. Their radical understandings of Christian discipleship were difficult even for other Christians to appreciate or tolerate. The Anabaptists also made a distinction between

Scholars can hardly wait until recess to try the snowy slopes.

church and state. If the state required something of its citizens that the Anabaptists thought was in conflict with the life and teachings of Jesus, they risked persecution and martydom rather than violating their consciences.

Peace and nonresistance were, and continue to be, major tenets of their faith. Jesus's life and teachings, they believe, call his followers to reject the use of violence.

Sunday afternoons allow time to walk to the neighbors for a visit.

Church is held on alternating Sundays in members' homes.

From their beginnings the Amish have realized that their interpretation of faithfulness to God results in misunderstanding, rejection by and separation from the world. Separation is a way of life for these people. Together, they have chosen guidelines and symbols to help them discern how to live as the Bible teaches. The Amish have carefully worked at the discipline of drawing lines. Before adopting a new practice or a recent technology, Amish leaders try to determine its possible effect on their community. Many outsiders find the location and weight of those resulting lines to be misplaced, hypocritical and unimportant. For the Amish, however, those choices serve as guides to keep them close to God, family and the church.

The Amish are not perfect. When a people set high goals for themselves as the result of a religious impetus and live out their commitments publically, they make themselves open to criticism. Because the larger world does not understand or share many of the Amish concerns and commitments, the Amish can appear out of touch and inconsistent. Sometimes they are. Many times the rest of society simply does not understand Amish intentions and goals.

The Amish are cautious on technology. Most Amish groups farm with horses and mules. Most do not have telephones in their homes and do not own cars. Many use diesel motors around the house and barn as their energy source. The Amish do not think technology is inherently wrong. Their concern is where it will lead them individually and as a church. If they farmed with tractors and had the advantage of unlimited power from commercial power companies, the temptations would be to get bigger and bigger and become more and more consumed with success. Cars, they believe, tend to break up the solidarity of the family. With cars, persons find it easy to get busier. Family members would soon be going in different directions, making it difficult for them to eat together regularly. The result, they reason, could be the gradual demise of the family unit.

Dress and language are additional highly visible distinctives of the Amish. Their dress is modest, simple and practical. Most is made at home using solid colored fabrics. Patterns are basic and devoid of frills and trends associated with current fashion. In addition to speaking English, most of the Amish groups speak a German dialect among themselves. Sociologically, language and dress strengthen group cohesiveness. One knows instantly who is part of the group and who is not. The Amish are not concerned with the social sciences; instead, their motivation is to be biblically faithful.

The Amish are cautious on extensive formal education. Most members of the groups complete their classroom studying with the eighth grade. The Amish observe that education has a way of making people think more highly of themselves than they should. Education also produces professionals who tend to move from the rural areas to distant cities. Such a move usually signals a significant weakening of one's community ties. For the Amish it is more important to belong to a community of faith than to be a rugged individualist. They believe that mutual accountability to the church is a more faithful way to live.

BASKETS

Baskets
Circa 1930–40 • Wool and rayon • 79 x 79 •
Lancaster Co., Pennsylvania • Dr. and Mrs.
Donald M. Herr.
Each pieced Basket has a small handle quilted
in the green triangle. The plain blue blocks are
filled with a quilted sunflower and the border
holds a winding rose quilting motif.

(below) **Baskets**
Circa 1925 • Cotton • 68 x 77 • Ohio • Judi
Boisson, Antique American Quilts, New York
City.
Though the quiltmaker used a variety of
fabrics in the pieced blocks, she placed them
skillfully to form crisp, sharp Basket patches.
Her careful attention to detail is also exhibited
in the graceful scroll-like quilting motif used in
the alternate plain blocks.

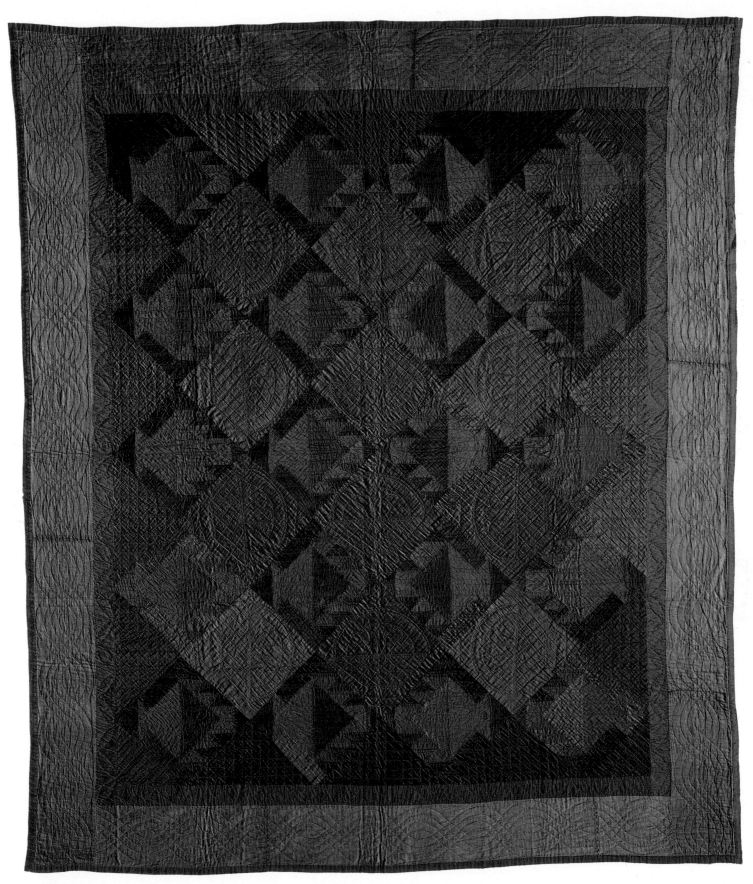

Baskets
Circa 1930 • Cotton • 72 x 85 • Ohio • Bettie Mintz, All of Us Americans Folk Art, Bethesda, MD.
Each plain square block dividing the pieced blocks is filled with a quilted Basket echoing the patchwork design. The quiltmaker, typical of many Ohio quilters from this period, chose to use only one color against a black background.

Baskets
Circa 1930 • Cotton • 71 x 71 • New Wilmington, Pennsylvania • Private collection.
Both piecework and quilting hold strictly to geometrics in the interior of this example. Trios of straight lines cross the Basket patches and tiny diamonds fill the plain patches. It is only on the outer border that the lines soften into curved heart shapes.

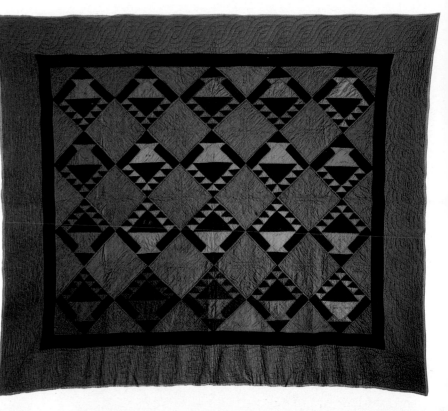

Baskets
Circa 1915 • Cotton • 62 x 72 • Goshen, Indiana • Collection of Barbara S. Janos • Made by Mrs. Levi Borntrager. Each pieced Basket holds the embroidered initials of a friend.

(below) **Baskets**
Circa 1938 • Cotton • 72 x 76 • Ohio • Diana Leone • This quilt is dated "March 4, 1938." A cable quilting motif surrounds this patchwork design. Along the top and bottom edges, the outer border is wide enough to accommodate the cable design. However, the side borders are more narrow, and the cable design extends into and fills the inner border along each side.

(above right) **Baskets**
Circa 1930–40 • Cotton • 73 x 88 • Holmes County, Ohio • Private collection.
The pieced Basket blocks in this quilt were made about 1930, but the quilt was not assembled and quilted until 1940.

Baskets
Circa 1930 • Cotton • 65 x 87 • Ohio • Jill
and Henry Barber.
Close examination shows that the piecework
on this quilt was not completely accurate in its
execution. Several of the blocks are uneven
and the shape of the total quilt is skewed.
However, the dazzling cotton sateen fabric and
the extra touch of the zigzag binding make it
an eye-catching example.

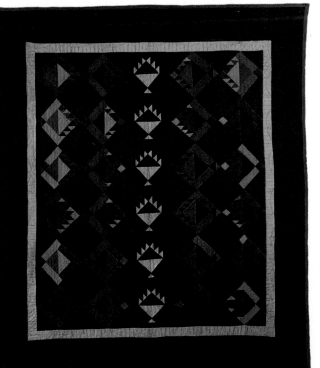

Baskets
Circa 1930 • Cotton • 68 x 78 • Ohio •
America Hurrah, New York City.
As with any patchwork design, the Basket in
this example is seen most clearly when the
fabrics stand in sharp contrast to each other.
The center row of Baskets is clear, but their
outline becomes less obvious in the outer rows.

Lady of the Lake
Circa 1930 • Cotton • 77 x 78 • Mifflin Co.,
Pennsylvania • Bettie Mintz, All of Us Americans Folk Art, Bethesda, MD.
This is a diversion from the typical blockwork
quilts of Mifflin Co. The four identical patches
in the center, anchored by the black pieced
patches in the corners, create the feeling of
a Center Square motif.

Lady of the Lake
Circa 1910 • Cotton • 65 x 78 • Southern
Indiana • Bettie Mintz, All of Us Americans
Folk Art, Bethesda, MD.
Although the piecework in this quilt is not
precisely planned, the quiltmaker did organize
it so that the colors run in diagonal lines
across the quilt top. A Chinese Coins inner
border using the four colors of the interior
frames the pieced blocks effectively.

Plain Quilts

Plain Quilt with inner border
Circa 1930 • Cotton • 67 x 77 • Ohio
Most quilts were made with one side clearly intended to be the top. Occasionally a quilt was constructed with a dominant pattern on one side and a simple design on the back. The result was a reversible quilt. This quilt has a double inner border on the top side. The back is identical except that the inner border is single.

(above) Plain Quilt or **Picture Frame**
1935 • Cotton • 60 x 76 • Indiana •
Bill Kulczycki.
What plain cloth quilts lacked in pieced designs they usually compensated for in exquisite quilting. This quilt, though not densely quilted, has a lovely trio of feather circles in the center and smaller feather wreaths in each corner. The border quilting is a cable design.

(above right) Plain Quilt with inner border
Circa 1925 • Cotton • 72 x 78 • Ohio • Bryce and Donna Hamilton.
In many Ohio quilts, the quilting took a back seat to the more dominant patchwork design. Plain quilts, however, used elaborate and extensive quilting. This example, although a plain cloth quilt, is decorated with a zigzag inner border and sawtooth binding.

Plain Quilt with double inner border
Circa 1930 • Cotton • 65 x 83 • Holmes Co., Ohio • Catherine Anthony.
Numerous quilting motifs were used to decorate Ohio quilts. This one is unique with its pineapple design.

BOW TIE

Bow Tie
Circa 1950 • Cotton and rayon • 69 x 87 •
Ohio • Judi Boisson, Antique American
Quilts, New York City.
Two colors set in straight rows make this
a simple, clean example of the Bow Tie
pattern.

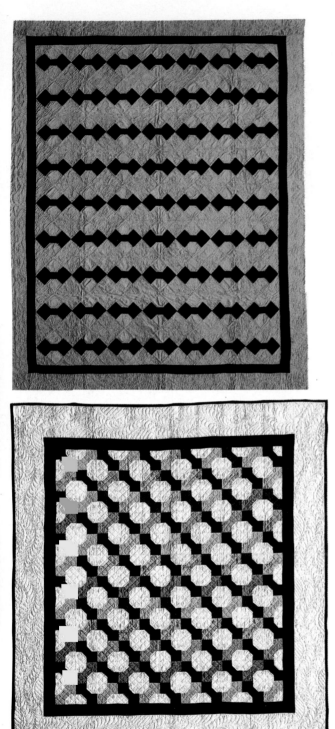

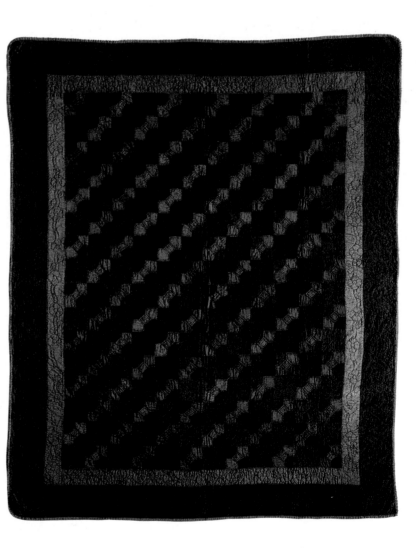

(*above left*) **Bow Tie**
Circa 1930 • Cotton • 72 x 79 • Ohio • Bryce and Donna Hamilton.
Dark blue and dark plum Bow Ties cut diagonally across this quilt in one direction, while lighter colors intersect
them in the opposite direction. The result is a negative space in an octagon shape. Fancy feather quilting fills the
outer border.

(*above right*) **Bow Tie**
Circa 1930 • Cotton and wool • 72 x 86 • Ohio • Penny Nii.
The Bow Ties in this quilt are all blue. However, the slight variation in the shades of blue, as well as shades in the
background fabric, add character to this somewhat weathered quilt.

Bow Tie
Circa 1915-20 • Cotton sateen and polished cotton • Approx. 73 x 80 • Holmes Co., Ohio • Barbara S. Janos.
This quilt was made by Mrs. Alvin Yoder, who obviously had a strong sense of color and design. The double inner border is anchored at each corner with a Four-Patch block. Each Bow Tie is filled with a small quilted tulip; a curved feather design graces the border.

MONKEY WRENCH

Monkey Wrench
Circa 1930 • Cotton sateen • 67 x 79 • New Wilmington, Somerset Co., Pennsylvania • Private collection.
This quilt literally shimmers with its combination of two colors in sateen weave. The rich looking fabric, together with the delicate feather quilting on its border, give this quilt a feeling of elegance.

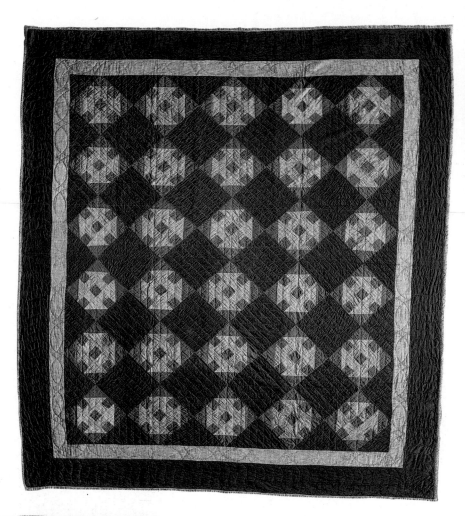

Monkey Wrench
Circa 1930 • Cotton • 72 x 82 • Holmes Co.,
Ohio • Private collection.
All patches except the one in the lower left
corner appear to be pieced from the same fabric. It would be interesting to know whether
the quiltmaker simply ran out of fabric
or whether she made the exception inten-
tionally.

Monkey Wrench
Circa 1920 • Cotton • 72 x 80 • Ohio •
Paulie Carlson.
This pattern is also known as Churn Dash and
Hole in the Barn Door.

PINWHEEL

(above) **Pinwheel**
Circa 1925 • Cotton • 65 x 77 • Mercer Co.,
PA • Bettie Mintz, All of Us Americans Folk
Art, Bethesda, MD.
Many of the families in the Amish settlement
in Mercer County trace their roots to Mifflin
County and have maintained connections with
their mother communities. This quilt shows
characteristics of Mifflin County in its flat, less
decorative quilting motifs, proportions and
color.

(above left) **Pinwheel**
1915 • Cotton • 75 x 87 • Holmes Co., Ohio
• Penny Nii.
The black cotton sateen used for the background reflects light differently, depending on
the direction of the grain of the fabric. This
results in slight variations in the lustre of the
background pieces, even though they are the
same fabric.

Pinwheel
Circa 1930 • Cotton • 80 x 80 • Holmes Co.,
Ohio • Private collection.
Both large and small Pinwheels seem to spin in
the piecework of this design. The appliqued
sawtooth binding complements the triangular
shapes inside it.

Pinwheel
Circa 1930 • Cotton • 76 x 79 • Ohio • Jill and Henry Barber.
Each leaf on the border of this quilt is double quilted, a pratice seldom used by Amish women today.

RAILROAD CROSSING

Railroad Crossing
Circa 1920 • Cotton • 65 x 89 • Holmes Co., Ohio • Judi Boisson, Antique American Quilts, New York City.
This is a relatively simple rendition of the Railroad Crossing. The scale of this particular pieced pattern is larger than many quilts done in this design. Its unusual combination of blue, brown tones and red make it aesthetically appealing.

Railroad Crossing
1921 • Cotton • 68 x 71 • Ohio
Intials "L.J.H." and the date "Feb. 17, 1921"
are quilted one on each side of the center star
in the black sashing.

Railroad Crossing
Circa 1920 • Cotton • 68 x 91 • Holmes Co.,
Ohio • Judi Boisson, Antique American
Quilts, New York City.
The piecework on this quilt demonstrates the
reason that the Railroad Crossing pattern is a
special one. Pieced stars mark the intersections
of each Crossing point and the pieced triangles
are tiny and well organized. This quiltmaker
added a double inner border to each side but
only a single one on the top and bottom.

DOUBLE WEDDING RING

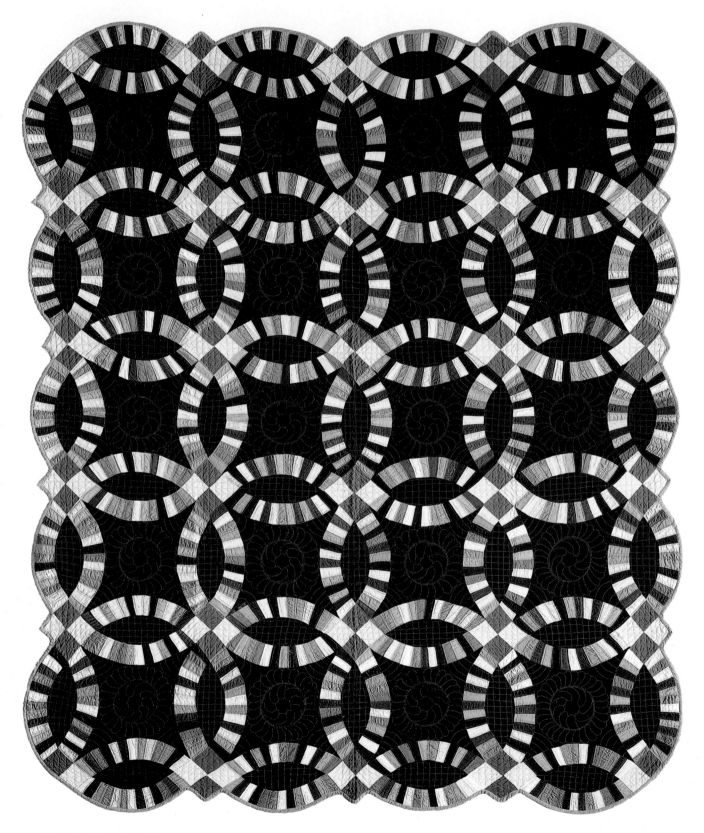

Double Wedding Ring
Circa 1930 • Cotton • 75 x 90 • Ohio • Judi Boisson, Antique American Quilts, New York City.
A multitude of colors dance on the black field of this quilt; the center of each Ring is filled with a quilted feather
circle. Scalloped edges on quilts became more popular with Amish quilters after 1940.

Double Wedding Ring
Circa 1915 • Cotton • 69 x 72 • Ohio • Judi
Boisson, Antique American Quilts, New
York City.
These circles appear to be floating on their
blue background. The use of black fabrics at
the intersection of each Ring ties them
together effectively.

Double Wedding Ring
Circa 1930 • Cotton • 65 x 73 • Ohio • Judi
Boisson, Antique American Quilts, New
York City.
Double Wedding Ring quilts were pieced in a
variety of ways. This one is set inside a square
with a Chinese Coins inner border.

FLOWER GARDEN

Flower Garden
Circa 1935-45 • Cotton and rayon • 77 x 80 • Ohio • Private collection.
A black inner border and the black centers on each of the Flowers have an overall darkening effect on a quilt that includes several pastel shades.

Flower Garden/Honeycomb
Circa 1930 • Cotton, wool and rayon • 86 x
94 • Ohio • Bettie Mintz, All of Us Americans
Folk Art, Bethesda, MD.
Matching the six sides of each hexagon makes
piecing the Flower Garden quilt a challenge for
any quiltmaker. This quilt also has mitered
corners on its borders, an additionally difficult
task.

Flower Garden
Circa 1930 • Cotton • 79 x 86 • Ohio
From the late 1930s on, Ohio quiltmakers
began using lighter colors. This example on
a white background is a clear example of the
transition away from the darker, more conservative quilts.

Bear Paw

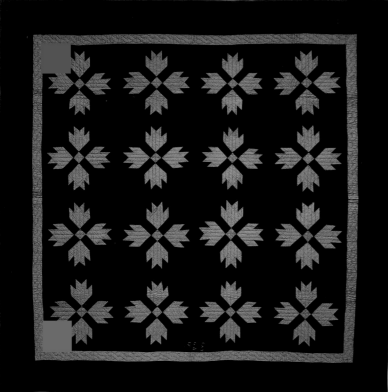

Bear Paw
1928 • Cotton sateen • 74 x 74 • Holmes Co.,
Ohio • Private collection • Made by
Fannie Hershberger.
The sharp, jagged edges of the Bear Paw
patches are softened by the graceful feather
wreath quilting in the open spaces. The border
continues the quilting theme with a meander-
ing feather wrapping the quilt.

Bear Paw
Circa 1930 • Cotton • Approx. 68 x 72 •
Indiana • America Hurrah, New York City.
There is a primitive, almost crude quality
about this quilt. Its pieced patches are not
perfect; several of the Bear Paw triangles are
turned so that the patches look more like Baskets; the quilting lines are unevenly spaced
and sometimes crooked. Yet the quilt's overall
effect, with its randomly spaced bright colors,
is cheerful and charming.

Bear Paw
1918 • Cotton • 68 x 85 • Mt. Hope, Holmes Co., Ohio • Catherine Anthony.
This quilt was made for Katie Miller Kurtz at her marriage; its current condition indicates that it was seldom used.
Although the quilting is only straight lines, it was made interesting by the quilter's decision to reverse the direction
of the lines on every other patch and to run them diagonally along the border.

ONE PATCH

Blockwork
1929 • Wool • 75 x 78 • Ontario, Canada • Privately owned • Initialed "R.E.B."
The yellow embroidery stitching which outlines the patches is of one type, although it varies significantly across the quilt top. Apparently it is the work of several different individuals.

One-Patch

1895 • Wool • 70 x 79 • Lancaster Co.,
Pennsylvania • Bettie Mintz, All of Us
Americans Folk Art, Bethesda, MD.
It is difficult to determine whether this is a
One-Patch quilt or a giant Nine-Patch with
borders. The center patch has the following
data in beautiful double-quilted script: "P.K.B.,
F.M.M., B.Z.Z., 1895, Lanc., PA."

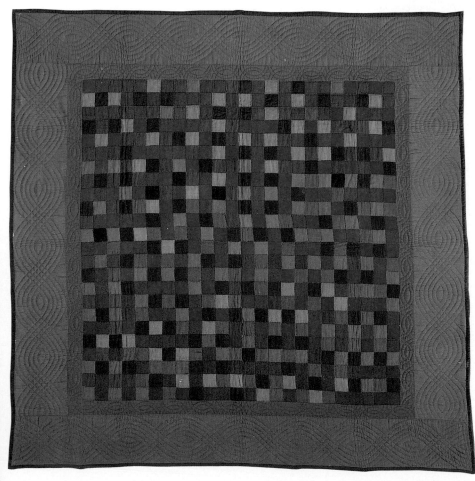

One-Patch

Circa 1930 • Wool • Approx. 71 x 71 • Ohio
• America Hurrah, New York City.
A bright blue inner border frames and gives
order to the randomly spaced squares in this
design.

"Millions of Stitches"

These comments about quilting appeared throughout the years in *Die Botschaft*, a periodical with many Amish correspondents and readers.

Women folks had a quilting yesterday here at our house. Seems quilting is quite popular these days. I have to wonder how many thousand quilts were made in Amish settlements over the USA in the last five yrs. I would imagine enough to cover a lot of acres! Millions of stitches! A lot of these were made to sell and also to pay dr. bills, etc.—Belfast, NY

On the 5th we had my side of the family here. We missed you Elam and Sally and family. So I hope to stick to sewing and quilting the rest of Dec. instead of baking cookies, etc. which I did in Nov.—Ronks, PA

On Wed. we were quilting at Jonas Fishers for our women driver, Virginia Baldwin. She's had radium treatments this fall for a cancer tumor in her lungs, now she was hospitalized last week due to bronchitis. She'd planned the quilting before she got sick again so we just went ahead anyway tho we wished she could have been with us. She is home from hospital again but tired and weak. We quilted a butterfly applique and a lone star, almost finishing the star, while the butterfly was done soon after noon.—Allenwood, PA

Today was the quilting at Melvin J. Byler's for the friendship quilt the shippers made for our milk man for Christmas.—Dayton, PA

Nancy S. Brenneman took her pupils to Nancy Y. Summy to sing Christmas songs and say their poems on Wed., Dec. 23. Nancy Summy has been a shut-in for a number of years already due to allergies. She appliques quilt blocks which gives her pass time and a little income but she can no longer stand it to knit.—Salisbury, PA

Quiltings are a no no in this column, but since the Mrs. had a small one, not a full blown hen party, guess you could call it only a chick party, as there were only a few select ones here at this no ordinary quilt. The patches were found after Daddy passed away and no one knows how old they are. Probably his mother or grandmother. Looks like it could be close to one hundred years old. Brown, grey, off red and something

Last year's crop was bigger than the barn.

that not everyone would want to put on their bed.— New Wilmington, PA

Yesterday my wife had a quilting. I just thought it's a good thing we don't have to buy grease to grease our mouth. I think it would have took a case that day. Of course, I think they enjoyed themselves. Gideon Lizzie was also helping.—Fort Plain, NY

Last night I put a quilt into frame. I find that quite a relaxing job these cold winter days. To those of you who do quilting, melt some parawax and put your quilting thread in it about 5 minutes, turn the spool every so often so it all gets covered evenly. Now you can enjoy quilting—your thread won't tangle and the needle even threads easier! Just try it! I wouldn't want to quilt any other way anymore. Colored threads will turn a shade darker.—Clyde, NY

Women and girls have sewing and quilting to see to. Replenishing the family's clothing supply will take a little while yet. After sewing 6 lined winter coats the next 3 to go shouldn't be too difficult. With so many projects going on and 3 sewing machines humming away, the house looks almost like a factory mixed in with living quarters!—Marion, KY

Yesterday we were all at mothers for the day. We finished a quilt and made 2 small comforts, besides making meals and taking care of the little ones.—Gordonville, PA

Thursday the 19th was the day of the 2nd quilting bee held in this area at Rudy L. Byler's. After being held up from quilt work during Jan. with their son Levi at Albany Hospital, the Newport folks sent word they would like to help a day. The women of our area could all be there but 2, so we had a good sized group working on 2 big quilts in one room, the 1st one started on was out of frame by 2 o'clock, and another put in. Thanks to the Newporters, they came early and stayed late. A lot of stitches made in one day.—Fort Plain, NY

Am looking for Emma Wengard today to start clean house, guess we'll start in attic. Her mother Mrs. Andy Wengard is having a quilting on Tues. Then on Fri. scholar moms and a few others to Alta Swarey for a quilting in de valley. Plowing has started and garden is being spade and few have seeds in.—Mifflintown, PA

This is the time of yr. for quiltins, frolics and moving, which we've had quite a few of. On Wed., sis. Sadie

Women are usually responsible for the gardens; however, the men help to prepare the ground before the seeds are planted.

(Daniel Lapps) moved close to Quarryville. Yest. we attended a frolic at bro. Aaron Zook's. Next week I have two quiltins to attend. It is hard to get house cleaned with so much agoing, so we did not start yet.—Leola, PA

Last week a quilting and manure hauling was held at Levi S. Borntreger's to help with bills.—Curtiss, WI

The work among the women folks is quilting and making rugs, while the men attend sales.—East Union, OH

The women are busy quilting and setting hens.—Montgomery, IN

Work among the men folks is working wood and hauling manure. The woman folk are busy quilting and keeping the stoves warm.—Haysville, OH

To Andy Yoder the Rexford, Mont. scribe about walking around the quilt for a few years. Maybe you could shorten the time by helping your wife quilt. You could be in by the stove where it is nice and warm. I have been helping my wife quilt almost 2 years. Occasionally she inspects my quilting.—Punxsutawney, PA

JACOB'S LADDER

Jacob's Ladder
Circa 1910 • Cotton sateen • 68 x 81 • Mifflin Co., Pennsylvania • Private collection.
The maker of this quilt, Mrs. Samuel Sharp, entitled it "Footprints in the Sands of Time."

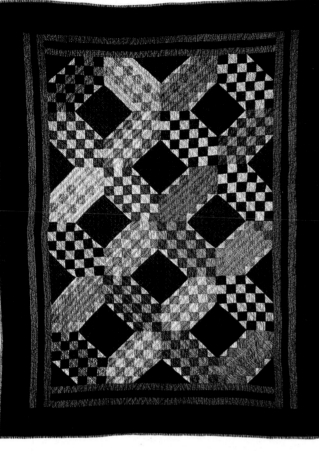

(above) **Jacob's Ladder Variation**
Circa 1935 • Cotton • 57 x 75 • Indiana •
Judi Boisson, Antique American Quilts, New
York City.
Though not truly a Jacob's Ladder quilt, this
variation has some of the feeling of that
pattern's upward climb. The split inner border
adds a unique touch to this quilt.

(above right) **Jacob's Ladder**
Circa 1910 • Cotton and wool • 69 x 81 •
Ohio • Barbara Janos • Made by Lucy
A. Yoder.
The blue and purple fabrics used in both the
blocks and background fabric are randomly
placed, yet create an active visual interplay.
Likely the quilter had scraps that were not
large enough for all the background triangles,
so she used them as well in the smaller
blocks.

Jacob's Ladder
Circa 1930 • Cotton • 67 x 76 • Ohio
This pattern is often done with the pieced
blocks tipped on an angle, creating a diagonal
rather than a vertical Ladder across the surface
of the quilt.

TRIANGLES

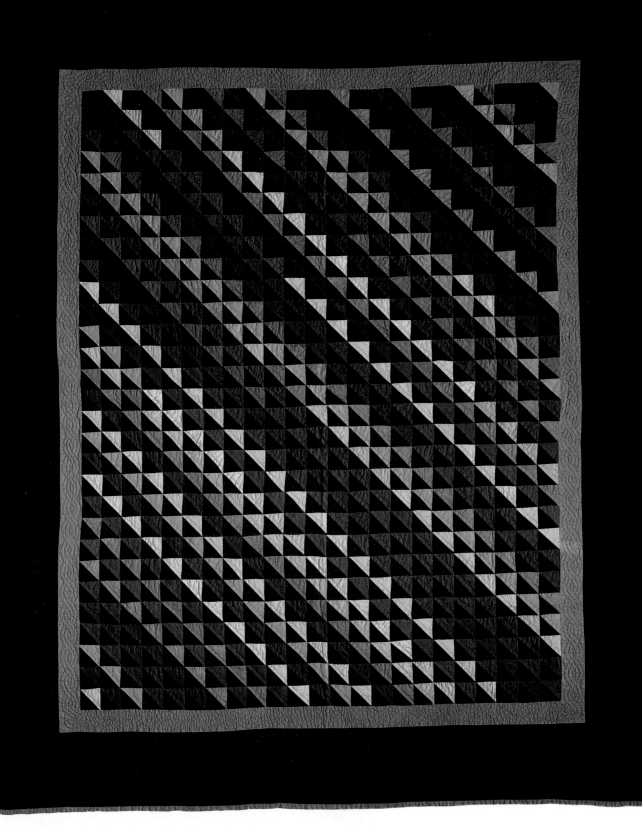

Triangles
Circa 1920 • Cotton • 68 x 80 • Holmes Co., Ohio • Private collection.
The alternate use of black and multicolored Triangles gives this quilt a great deal of energy. It is, however, dutifully restrained within its double border.

Triangles
Circa 1930 • Cotton • 61 x 77 • Ohio • Judi Boisson, Antique American Quilts, New York City.
It appears that the quiltmaker constructed this quilt in halves and then joined them in the center. In the more traditional variation of this pattern, all the Triangles run in the same direction.

Zigzag Triangles
Circa 1920 • Cotton • 65 x 72 • Ohio • Jill and Henry Barber.
Although it is now showing signs of deterioration, this quilt was originally a vibrant and lovely masterpiece.

BROKEN DISHES

Broken Dishes
Circa 1930 • Cotton • Approx. 75 x 84 •
Ohio • America Hurrah, New York City.
A beautiful fiddlehead fern quilting motif is
used on the outer border of this quilt.

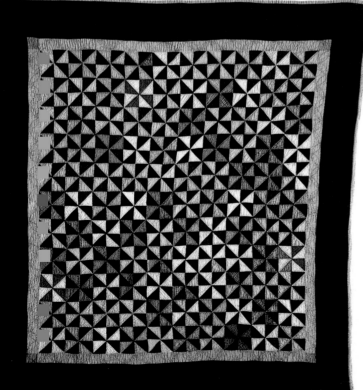

Broken Dishes
Circa 1915 • Cotton • 64 x 71 • Ohio •
Private collection.
The consistent placement of black fabric
creates a pinwheel effect in this pattern. The
use of an inner border is very common in
Ohio quilts but the green corner blocks are
unusual. Corner blocks are very common in
quilts of Lancaster Co., PA but are found less
frequently in quilts from other Amish communities.

Broken Dishes
Circa 1930 • Cotton • 74 x 84 • Ohio • Bryce and Donna Hamilton.
The bright yellow fabric which gives this quilt its spark was permitted by many midwestern Amish groups, but was seldom used by the Amish quiltmakers of Lancaster County.

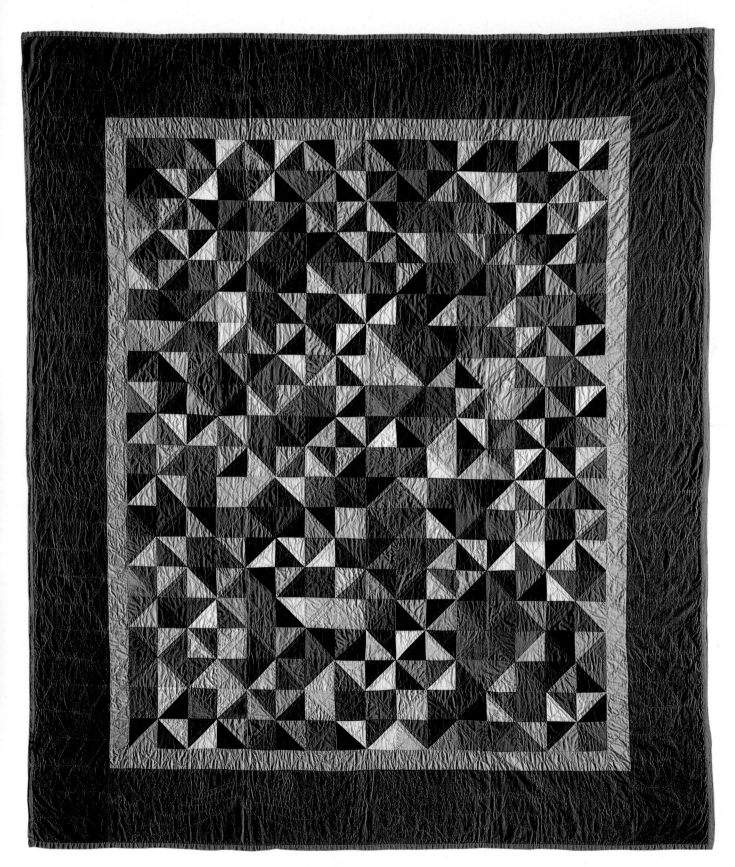

Broken Dishes
1937 • Cotton • 64 x 75 • Holmes Co., Ohio • Catherine Anthony.
Today, as in years gone by, most Amish girls have several quilts in their hope chests by the time they are of marriage age. Some of these are made for them by family members, and some are the work of their own hands. This quilt was made for Lydiann Miller as one of her wedding quilts.

Broken Dishes
Circa 1925 • Cotton • 71 x 77 • Ohio •
Judi Boisson, Antique American Quilts,
New York City.
The quilter responsible for making this quilt
did not take the easy way out. She increased
the challenge of this otherwise simple pattern
by leaving a zigzag edge along the pieced
blocks and by adding a sawtooth binding.

(below right) **Broken Dishes**
Circa 1920 • Cotton • 66 x 77 • Ohio • Judi
Boisson, Antique American Quilts, New
York City.
Several quilt patterns have more than one
name and are labelled differently by individual
quilters. This quilt is sometimes called Cups
and Saucers.

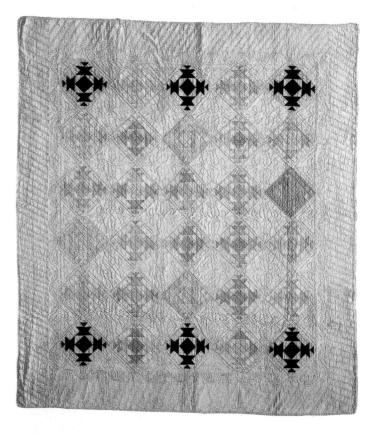

Broken Dishes
Circa 1920 • Cotton • 68 x 86 • Ohio • Judi Boisson, Antique American Quilts, New York City.
A double inner border along the top and bottom edges helps to increase the length of this quilt and enhance its
proportions as a bedcover.

*F*AN

Fan
Circa 1930–40 • Wool • Approx. 72 x 90 •
Ohio • America Hurrah, New York City.
Pairs of Fan patches are joined in this quilt to
form half circles in horizontal rows across the
quilt. This is technically not a quilt since it has
no quilting to connect the layers. In the
construction of the cover, the Fan sections are
connected to a fabric backing with no layer of
batting between. Because of that, and the fact
that there is no border, quilting was less neces-
sary.

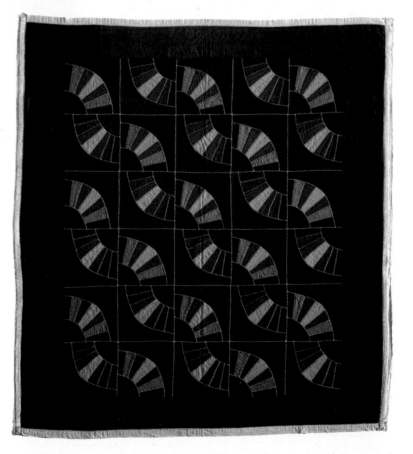

Fan
Circa 1930–40 • Cotton and rayon • 68 x 74 •
Ohio • Jill and Henry Barber.
The wide binding on this Fan is typical of
Lancaster Co., PA quilts. However, the black
background and the quilting designs indicate a
more midwestern influence. Likely the quilt
was made in Ohio or Indiana by a quilter who
had recently moved from Lancaster and
retained her method of binding.